1983

THE STRANGEST CASES ON RECORD

STATE OF OHIO,)
) ss.   IN THE MUNICIPAL COURT.
CUYAHOGA COUNTY.)

56583

Edwin Hains,   )
     Plaintiff,   )
)
     vs.   )   STATEMENT OF CLAIM.
)
William M. Duncan,   )
Receiver of The Wheeling)
& Lake Erie Railroad Company,)
)
     Defendant.   )

Now comes the plaintiff, Edwin Hains, and prays this august Court
  To heed the very earnest plea, enshrined in this report.
The Wheeling & Lake Erie Railroad Company, a heartless corporation,
  But licensed under certain laws of this fair State and Nation;
Did, by a spark through carelessness, from a locomotive owned
  By the defendant in this Court, and by it not atoned,
Destroy and render Null and Void, a building situate
  Upon the rear of premises, known as E. Hains Estate,
Which in the town of Bedford lies, a placid rural spot,
  Until the conflagration, which spoiled the plaintiff's lot,
The second of November last was the most woeful date
  On which the said defendant did this outrage perpetrate.
Said building being plain but good, and open to all callers,
  Was worth in money of the realm, the sum of fifty dollars.
Now, the aforesaid Hains will not cite Blackstone Coke or Livy,
  The incinerated building was, in vulgar terms a privy.
The wealthy have from two to eight, but this case is more sad,
  For like the poor man's one ewe lamb, 'twas the only one he had.
And now in frigid winter time, before beginning labor,
  He eke perforce must use the can of an obliging neighbor.

The plaintiff does still further state that he is an inventor,
  And since the late catastrophy he has no place to center
His great inventive genius which, before in chaste seclusion
  Of the before in mentioned can, did blossom in profusion.
True genius cannot be appraised, but plaintiff's was so nifty,
  He thinks he should receive therefor at least one hundred fifty.
He therefore prays the Court to grant, two hundred Iron Men,
  That he may once more take his place midst Bedford's upper ten,
And walk abroad midst citizens, and meet them man to man,
  Which now he cannot rightly do, he being shy a can.
And so he prays that he may go from hence with compensation,
  Commensurate with what he's lost, through this his degredation.
And so he windeth up his prayer, and hopes the court will grant
  One hundred fifty for his peace of mind, and fifty for the plant.

Edwin Hains

State of Ohio,
Cuyahoga County, ss.
    Sworn to and subscribed in my presence this 1st day of June, 1916.

Chas H Gensemey
                          Deputy Clerk.

THE
STRANGEST
CASES

ON RECORD

by

JOHN ALLISON DUNCAN

Member of the Bar of the State of Ohio

Illustrated by the Author

REILLY & LEE · CHICAGO

TO MY DEAR WIFE

PHYLLIS

*who made many helpful suggestions
while this book was being written*

As crafty lawyers to acquire applause
Try various arts to get a double cause,
    So does an author, rummaging his brain
By various methods, try to entertain.

PASQUIN

THE first curiosity in the law which crossed my path was the poetic petition (frontispiece) which was filed against the receiver of the Wheeling & Lake Erie Railroad Company. One of the deputies in the Clerk's Office told me about it. He had committed it to memory and took delight in quoting it. To me it seemed one of the funniest pleadings ever filed in a court of law. The author, Edson Hains, was not a lawyer but apparently was qualified to plead his own cause. Trial was held in Cleveland, on December 26, 1916, before Judge William H. McGannon, who, after a full hearing, decided in favor of the plaintiff Hains. He assessed the Railroad Company twenty-five dollars and costs for negligently causing a spark to travel from one of its locomotives to Mr. Hains' field in Bedford, Ohio, and eventually to his outhouse, reducing it to ashes. In the choice language of the pleader, who would not "cite Blackstone, Coke or Livy, the incinerated building was, in vulgar terms, a privy," which Mr. Hains regarded as "so nifty" as to be worth "one hundred fifty." The plaintiff added that "he was an inventor, and since the late catastrophy, he had no place to center." All the essential elements are contained in this very amusing rhymed petition.[1]

At first I did not believe there was any such pleading on record and I was more than pleased when I found the original statement of claim in the files on the fourth floor of the Cleveland City Hall. I obtained permission to take my first legal oddity out of the courthouse and have it photostated. I returned it to the file room, but years later when I looked for it again, it was gone. Just where the original is now, I don't know. What I do know is that finding it started me on a search for "queeriosities" of the law. I venture to say that I have read over three hundred books to furnish the basis for this volume. True, some of my lawyer friends have been very helpful in digging out curios, and to them I am truly grateful.

Many rare gems were discovered quite accidentally. In briefing some serious question of law, a legal freak would "put itself above the horizon." More often, however, one legal curiosity led to another. This has been especially true in connection with wills. There is such a dearth of oddity in the field of law generally, that it has often been like looking for the proverbial needle in a haystack. However, I found more than I expected. The legal profession should be ashamed to think it has been partially responsible for as much "loony law" as there is. It is nothing to be proud of. If this work does nothing more than inform the barristers of the world of "screwball" legislation and decisions, I shall feel that I have accomplished something.

The freak wills, of course, are not the work of lawyers, and the legal profession must not be blamed for such foolish bequests and devises as are found in Chapter VIII.

I have not intended to provoke any ill feeling against the Bar. My only purpose has been to entertain.

JOHN A. DUNCAN

Cleveland, Ohio

CONTENTS

CHAPTER   PAGE

1. CRIMES THAT NEVER HAPPENED   15

   Beggar Monrousseau; Convicted of Self-Murder; The Boorn Brothers
   Case; Lincoln's Defense of Innocent "Murderers"

2. ANIMAL TRIALS   27

   The Trial of the Weevils; The Trial of the Ants; The Trial of the
   Mosquitoes; Trials of Caterpillars, Locusts, Flies and Crickets; Eels'
   Rights; Excommunication of Doves; Leeches Brought to Justice; Grass-
   hoppers and a Dead Lawyer; The Rooster Sorcerer; Pigs on Trial; Rats
   up for Burglary; A Bull Murderer; A Bear Jury?; Convictions of Cows;
   A Sacrilegious Donkey; Prosecuted Horses; Criminal Roosters—1938;
   A Blue Law and a Monkey; Recent Animal Convictions

3. POSTHUMOUS TRIALS   44

   Pope Formosus; Thomas À Becket

4. CELEBRATED CASES OF HISTORY   49

   The Egyptian Mummy Case; Disputed Identity; Roulette Winnings;
   The Tichborne Imposters; Rope Justice; Captain Kidd's Execution;
   The Dred Scott Decision; Patient v. Doctor; The Dutch Nation In-
   dicted; Christopher Columbus' Trial; The Bidwell Gang in London;
   Galileo's Perjury; Joan of Arc as Lawyer; A Seven-Year Trial; Socrates
   v. Athens; The Haymarket Square Case; The Longest Civil Case

5. JUDICIAL HUMOR   66

   The Wittiest Judge; Hoss Sense; Self-Defense; Crude Wit; The Shortest Charges; Consider Your Verdict; The High Cost of Law; "The
   Reasonable Doubt"

6. PECULIAR PENALTIES   76

A Bigamist's Punishment; Penalty Without Crime; Penalty of Silence; Head Plowing; Women Who Quarrel; Consistency—Hobgoblin of

Judges; Work or Die; Original Pole-Sitters; Threatened Greek Legislators; Penalties of Jurors; Penalized for Extravagant Apparel; Thou Shalt Not Bear False Witness; Punishment of the Chinese Idols; Punishment of Marble Statues; Plowshare Punishment; The Metal Bridle; Head Baskets; Traveling on the Sabbath; Punishment of Huguenots; Book Burning; German Petty Offenders; Forfeit of "Mister"; Milk Drinking; Roger Bacon's Punishment; William Penn's Punishment; Voltaire's Punishment; The Guillotiner Guillotined; Pressing for an Answer; A Rifle Sentenced; The Punishment That Made a Lawyer; Massachusetts Punishments; Cardinal Wolsey's Punishment; An Author Forced To Eat His Own Words; Sadism?; Trespassers "Persecuted"

7. ODD DOCUMENTS   96

An Arizona Arrest; Deeded to God; Deeded to Jehovah God; Sir Francis Drake's Brass Plate; The World's Longest Lease; A Steel Check; A Wooden Check; A Cloth Check; A Two-Volume Complaint; A Poetic Brief; Cruikshank's Bank Note; An Expensive Bonfire; The World's Longest Deed; Property Traced to Adam and Eve; A Retroactive Marriage License; The Noah's Ark Exploration Association; Mr. Philpotts Changes His Name; A Razor-Back on a Railroad Track; The Smallest Real Estate Transaction in History

8. FREAK WILLS   121

Revenge in a Will; Estate Willed to Lord Jesus; Ancient Wills; Job's Will; Roman Views on Wills; Wills of Famous People; Eccentricity v. Insanity; Jeremy Bentham's Will; White Linen Clothes; Floral Rentals; Dissent; Drink the Sea; Shakespeare's Will; A Light Forever Burning; Intentionally; No Funeral Bell; Above Ground; Poetic Will; A Bequeathed Dinner; Not a Farthing If They Married; Cynical Provisions; To a Clean-Shaven Son; Willed to the Dead; Suspense; The Pledges of John Hedges; Animal Beneficiaries; Thirty Sous to Cats; A Libelous Will; Petticoat Will; Wills on Eccentric Materials; The Williston Fish Will; A Defiant Will; No Funeral Expense; A Smoker's Will; A Guarded Beard; A Woman-Hater's Will; Yorick's Skull; Preserved Skulls; Preserved Organs; Drumheads; An Idol Heir; A Clause For Lawyers; A Will in Shorthand; Phonograph-Record Evidence; Ballad on Wills

9. UNCOMMON LAW   158

Sanctuaries for Criminals; The "Neck Verse"; No Witnesses; Family Revenge; No Complaint Without a Witness; The Whole Town a Judge; Transfer of Property; Juries Then and Now; A Free Bite

10. ANCIENT METHODS OF TRIAL   168

Trial by Bier; A Method for Civil Cases; Oaths; Knife Trials; Compurgation; Trial by Hot Water; The Cold-Water Trial; Trial by Combat

11. LUDICROUS LAWS   183

Kansas Automobile Statute; A Change in Pi; All Trains Stopped Permanently; Land Limitations; Judges Penalized; No Manual Labor; Required Drunkenness; Crime to Kill Fairies; Prohibition of Beards; Roquefort Cheese Requirements; Streets Blocked by Churches; Leap Year Enforced; Christmas Prohibited in Massachusetts; Christmas Prohibited; The Bull of Adrian; Food Restrictions; Feminine Embellishments Forbidden; The Price of a Wife in Virginia; United States Legal Measure; Massachusetts Blue Laws; Distribution of Lawyers; No Women Smokers in New York; Mary Walker's Trousers; The Congressional Record Honors a Georgian; When Is a Lawyer a Fish?; No English Authorities; Unconscious Lawlessness; Food in English; Smallest Check; Chief Justice Dixon's Irony

12. UNUSUAL CHARACTERS IN THE LAW   199

Demosthenes; Saint Ives; Egotism; Stephen John Field; A Court Filibuster; Judgments from His Bed; Animal Defender; William Blackstone; Persistence; Twenty Thousand Death Sentences; Highwayman Judge; Disraeli; The World's Largest Political Meeting; The Longest Question; Another Long One; Lawyers' Fees; Law-Phobia; Rats!; A Courageous Judge

13. ECCENTRIC DECISIONS   214

Methuselah of the Law; A Disturbing Singer; United States v. 350 Cartons of Canned Sardines; Lawyers Can Cry; Judges' Gems; Damages for Barking Dogs; Shakespeare Not the Author; Imaginary Law Suit; Testimony of a Ghost; The Barber and His Tools; A Golfing Judge; A Beggar and His Legs; A Corporation's Alienation of Affections; Parrots and Contract Bridge; Texas Court Believes in Santa Claus; Not Guilty But Escaped

CHAPTER   PAGE

14. LEGAL GEMS   241

The Code of Hammurabi; The Case of the Cat's Legs; The Doghouse
Club; Strings Tied to Judgments; Spain's Longest Lawsuit; Lawyers'
Names; The Highest Money Judgment; A Pig Poem; Court Humor;
Judges on Delicate Subjects; Words in Litigation; Comic-Strip Char-
acters; Epigrammatic Judges; A Witty Opinion; All the Law and the
Gospels; Trademarks; Supreme Court Gems; Lincoln on Too Much
Talk; The Amiable Judge Sutherland; Window Blinds; "Concerning
Lawyers"; Twelve Men Good and True

15. OF LAW, OF TIME AND EPITAPHS   261

The Honest Solicitor; A Lover of Peace; Sir John Strange's Epitaph;
A Jaded Joke; A Bad Beginning; Client v. Lawyer; Rembrandt; Never
Too Old To Be Punished; Conclusion

INDEX   269

CHAPTER 1

CRIMES THAT NEVER HAPPENED

"Law is like a book of surgery—there are a great many terrible cases in it."
—From a Legal Satirist

MANY people have supposed that innocent men are never convicted. In fact, only recently a district attorney in Worcester County, Massachusetts, ventured: "Don't worry about it, it never happens in the world."[1]

Such a supposition, however, is absolutely groundless, for there are reported literally hundreds of cases here and abroad, involving the trial and conviction of perfectly innocent men. Just how many wrongfully convicted persons have been executed is difficult to say. In many cases where a murder allegedly took place, no crime in fact was ever committed. Nobody was murdered at all. Many times, records have shown the eventual return of the person supposedly murdered.

BEGGAR MONROUSSEAU

One of the earliest recorded cases of convicting the innocent was cited by Horace W. Fuller of the Suffolk Bar in his *Impostors and Adventurers*. There he related the sad case of a French beggar named Jean Monrousseau who was imprisoned

15

and put in irons for perpetrating a crime that never happened. In July, 1655, Monrousseau was in the town of Vernon, France. With him was a little boy whom many villagers erroneously recognized as Jacques le Moine, the long-lost son of Madame Jeanne le Moine.

From July 26th to the 12th of August, the judges of Vernon received evidence. During the course of investigation and trial, public indignation ran so high that Madame le Moine, fearful of her life, fled to Paris. Monrousseau alone insisted that the boy was his own son Louis. However, twenty-one witnesses insisted otherwise. Conviction followed and "by a judgment rendered by the Lieutenant General, it was directed that Monrousseau should be detained in prison, in chains, and that the child in litigation should be named Jacques le Moine—the judgment in this regard to take the place of a baptismal record; that the relatives of the said Jacques le Moine should be convoked to name a guardian for him, and an allowance of one hundred livres should be assigned him; and to effect this, the judgment authorized the seizure of all the property of the mother le Moine."

Hence, in the name of the Procureur du Roi, all the property of Madame le Moine was seized. From the judgment entered in Vernon she appealed to the Parliament of Paris and finally by petition to the Privy Council, stoutly denying that the beggar's boy was her own but that her son, Jacques, who had disappeared with his older brother, Pierre le Moine, had never returned. The illustrious avocat, Guillaume de Lamoignon, respected friend of Louis XIV, was retained by Madame le Moine to represent her on appeal.

On February 18, 1656, beggar Monrousseau was ordered by Privy Council decree to be removed to the prison in Paris. The case was reopened on June 2 of that year before the Parliament of Paris. In the midst of that hearing, "the folly of the judges of Vernon was made to appear as clear as the noonday sun." Madame le Moine's older son, Pierre, returned. He testified that his little brother, Jacques, had fallen sick at Saint-Waast and died some years before, having been buried in the church cemetery. In support of his testimony, Pierre offered in evidence "two certificates signed by the curé, by the vicar, and many inhabitants of the parish, and by those who had conducted the burial." The case was open and shut. The evidence stood uncontradicted. But "notwithstanding the opinion of the magistrates already formed as to the innocence of Monrousseau, as it was an unheard-of thing to mitigate the lot of a man accused of a crime, *however unjustly*, the beggar remained in prison." Legal historians add that "those who know what a prison was under Louis XIV can pity this poor fellow—a victim of the infatuation of his judges."

The Parliament of Paris did not take up the matter until the spring of 1659. Despite the overwhelming evidence in favor of Monrousseau, the case had been allowed to drag along. Finally, after the urgent pleas of even the advocate general, M. Bignon, Jean Monrousseau, the beggar, was ordered released from prison and his son returned to him.

The record of his imprisonment was stricken from the registry by way of atonement for this horrible mistake. Thus ended the remarkable case of a man who was convicted of a crime which in fact never existed. The boy he supposedly kidnapped was his own son. This remarkable case stands as a classic in the field of criminal law. Soon after it was decided, the leading jurists of France turned their thoughts toward ways of indemnifying innocent persons erroneously convicted.[2]

CONVICTED OF SELF-MURDER

Paul Hubert's case was another blot on the French annals of legal history. According to Robert L. Ripley of *Believe It or Not* fame, "Paul Hubert was convicted of murdering himself." This unusual case is recounted by Mr. Ripley in his first *Believe It or Not* book, as follows:[3]

"Paul Hubert was convicted of first degree murder by a 'Cour Correctionelle' of Bordeaux, France, and sentenced to death. The sentence was commuted to lifelong imprisonment and he was sent to the French penal colony in Guiana.

"In 1860, after he had served 21 years in solitary confinement, the Procureur Imperial moved the French Cour de

Cassation to review the case. The case was reopened and Hubert acquitted after the highest French Court found that his supposed victim was none other than himself!

"The Hubert case is a 'cause célèbre,' and a great argument for those who strive to abolish capital punishment."

A movement for indemnification was started in France toward the end of the eighteenth century. Voltaire was one of the champions of the cause; he secured the acquittal and restoration of the rights of De la Barre, Calas, and many others. The great satirist prevailed upon his good friend, Frederick the Great of Prussia, who decreed in 1766:

"If a person suspected of crime has been detained for trial, and where, for lack of proof, he has been released from custody, and in the course of time his complete innocence is established, he shall have not only complete costs restored to him, but also a sum of money as just indemnity, according to all the circumstances of the case, payable from the funds of the trial court, so that the innocent person may be compensated for the injuries he has suffered."[4]

Only within the last fifty years have European countries enacted legislation which indemnifies innocent victims of the errors of criminal justice, says Professor Borchard in *Convicting the Innocent*.

England has never legislated in this respect, although Parliament has on numerous occasions "granted lump sum indemnities as a matter of grace to various innocent individuals released after having suffered imprisonment upon erroneous conviction."[5]

A movement was begun in the United States in 1913 with

19

a view to indemnifying innocent victims who were unjustly convicted of crime; but to date, this type of much-needed legislation has not been acted upon. The states of California, North Dakota, and Wisconsin, however, have adopted statutes which make indemnification possible to some degree, says Professor Borchard.

THE BOORN BROTHERS CASE

The trial of Stephen and Jesse Boorn in Manchester, Vermont, is a classic in American jurisprudence. In May of 1812, the Boorn brothers had quarreled with Russel Colvin, their brother-in-law, who immediately disappeared. As time passed the townspeople became suspicious, and seven years later, after some of the personal effects of the alleged decedent were found on the Boorn homestead, the grand jury concluded that Jesse Boorn must have murdered his brother-in-law. Jesse stoutly denied his guilt but placed the blame on his brother Stephen. Both brothers were thrown in jail.

Their trial came up in November of 1819. The key witness for the state was a prison inmate who testified that Jesse had confessed to him in jail that Stephen Boorn had fractured the decedent's skull and later, with the aid of Jesse and their father, Barney Boorn, had slit his throat and buried the remains in the cellar; and that later an attempt was made to get rid of the evidence. Despite able counsel, the defense was unsuccessful and a verdict of guilty was returned. It is said that the jury was guided in its decision by what the defendants' old uncle, Amos Boorn, had said he had dreamed in the spring of 1819. The murdered man had supposedly come to his bedside three different times and told him that the Boorn brothers had killed him and buried his bones in the cellar, but later hid them in an old stump near the farmhouse. This prompted a finding of some bones which were at first summarily pronounced human but later discredited as such.

The Boorn brothers were sentenced to hang on January 28, 1820. Jesse's sentence was commuted to life imprisonment. Fortunately, Stephen reduced his sentence to an eventual acquittal, and, on November 29, 1819, he advertised in the *Rutland Herald* for the murdered man. The "ad" was reprinted in the *New York Evening Post*, which was read aloud in a New York hotel lobby by a former resident of Manchester in the presence of Tabor Chadwick, who remembered that a man answering Colvin's description was living with his brother-in-law in Dover, New Jersey. It was with much difficulty that the "murdered" man was persuaded to return to his home town and reveal his identity. His arrival was quite an event. After being greeted by friends and neighbors, Colvin was brought face to face with his brother-in-law, Stephen. When he asked why Stephen had on fetters, he received the reply, "Because they say I murdered you."

The case was then promptly reopened and the Boorn brothers were granted permission to enter new pleas. The State's Attorney quickly entered a *nolle prosequi* and both brothers were set free. Several months later they applied to the Vermont Legislature for compensation for the wrongful imprisonment and the suffering endured while in jail. Relief was refused and no indemnity was ever afforded the innocent brothers who might have swung on the gallows had they not advertised for the missing man whose whereabouts were accidentally revealed by a total stranger.[6]

LINCOLN'S DEFENSE OF INNOCENT "MURDERERS"

Abraham Lincoln and Stephen Trigg Logan had been in partnership hardly a month when they found themselves engaged in the most singular case that Lincoln ever tried.

In 1829, William, Henry, and Archibald Trailor moved from Kentucky to Springfield, Illinois. An eccentric school teacher named Archibald Fisher came to live with William Trailor about a hundred miles northwest of Springfield. He had accumulated several hundred dollars which he refused to deposit in a bank. In the latter part of May, 1841, William Trailor and Fisher started for Springfield, picking up Henry Trailor at Clary's Grove, and arriving in Springfield on July 1. They stopped at Archibald Trailor's boarding house, and after dinner the three brothers and Fisher took a stroll. The Trailors returned to the boarding house about supper time without their friend Fisher. They explained that, as they were walking along the footpath on the outskirts of town, Fisher had dropped behind and disappeared, not to be seen again. Many efforts were made to locate the missing man, but all without success. In the midst of the search William and Henry left the city for their homes.

On June 12th, the postmaster of Springfield received a letter from the postmaster at Greenbush in Warren County to the effect that William Trailor had come home and was boasting that Fisher had left him $1500.00. Residents of Springfield became highly enraged and demanded the immediate arrest of the Trailors. Soon after, Henry was arrested and, while in the Springfield jail, was put through a "third degree" by the Mayor and Josiah Lamborn, the Attorney General. Three days later, Henry weakened under the tremendous strain and confessed that his two brothers, William and Archibald, had murdered Fisher, concealing the body in a woods and later throwing it in Hickox's Millpond a short distance away.

William and Archibald Trailor were immediately taken

into custody and placed under heavy guard. Henry Trailor's confession caused tremendous excitement and the murder became the main topic of the day. Storekeepers suspended their business, forming parties to scour the woods and collect every available piece of circumstantial evidence. The towns-people chopped down the mill dam, over the owner's protest, in an effort to locate the school teacher's remains.

William Trailor took the stand on June 18th. Curious townspeople literally packed the courtroom to capacity. Josiah Lamborn, Attorney General of the State, was in charge of the prosecution. Between Logan and Lincoln sat Archibald and William Trailor. The first witness for the State was Henry Trailor, who repeated his confession. The defense was unable to break him on cross-examination.

The next witness to take the stand was a lady who had known the Trailors many years. She testified that she saw the Trailor brothers with Fisher on the day he disappeared; that they went into the woods and a short time later she saw the Trailors leave the woods alone. It was proved by other wit-nesses that where they had entered the woods there was evi-dence of a terrific struggle. A club with hair on it had been found in that vicinity. A doctor, after a long scientific exami-nation, pronounced the hair to be human whiskers such as Fisher wore. Tracks were said to be found which led to the pond at Hickox's Mill, indicating that a buggy had been driven into the water and then backed out. The situation appeared hopeless for the Trailors. They had no air-tight defense at all and the confession fairly clinched the case.

Suddenly something happened. Lincoln slowly arose and

stated that the defense desired to introduce only one witness. A white-haired old gentleman by the name of Dr. Gilmore, who bore a very fine reputation, was then called to the stand.

The doctor testified that Fisher—the one who was supposed to be dead—was not dead but very much alive, and that he was at that very moment in the doctor's home in a near-by county. He said that, several years before, Fisher had been badly injured by a gun exploding near his head, and since that time had been subject to occasional loss of memory. He stated that several days after the alleged murder, he had found Fisher wandering near his home in Warren County, suffering a complete lapse of memory. The doctor's testimony caused the case to take a dramatic turn. The Trailor brothers were immediately released from custody. Judge Logan was forced to jump up on a table and calm the crowd of spectators who suddenly turned against the Attorney General who had wrung out the false confession. In a few days Fisher returned, apparently fully recovered, and repeated the facts of his strange disappearance. The whiskers on the club were later discovered to be cow hairs, and the woods where the struggle allegedly took place was where school children had attempted to hang a rope swing.

The day after the trial (June 19, 1841), Lincoln sat down and wrote his friend, Joshua Speed, in Louisville, saying:

"When the Doctor's story was first made public, it was amusing to scan and contemplate the countenances and hear remarks of those who had been actually in search of the dead body; some looked comical, some melancholy and some furiously angry. Porter, who had been very active, swore he

25

always knew the man was not dead and that he had not stirred an inch to hunt for him; Langford, who had taken the lead in cutting down Hickox's mill dam and wanted to hang Hickox for objecting, looked most awfully woe-begone; he seemed the victim of 'unrequited affection' as was represented in the comic almanacs we used to laugh over, and Hart, the little drayman that hauled Molly home once said that it was too *damn* bad to have so much trouble and no hanging after all."[7]

Historian Carl Sandburg tells us that the Trailors died four years later without paying Lincoln for his legal services, and the future President was obliged to sue their estate in order to collect his hundred-dollar fee "for services rendered."[8]

SOURCES

Chapter 1

1. Convicting the Innocent, by Edwin Borchard, preface, p. vii, Yale University Press.

2. Impostors and Adventurers, by Horace W. Fuller, Soule & Bugbee, pp. 143-168.

3. Believe It or Not, by Robert L. Ripley, Simon & Schuster, p. 26.

4. Convicting the Innocent, by Edwin Borchard, Yale University Press.

5. Convicting the Innocent, by Edwin Borchard, Yale University Press.

6. Trial of Stephen and Jesse Boorn for the murder of Russel Colvin (Rutland, Vt.; Fay & Burt, 1820).
   Convicting the Innocent, by Edwin Borchard, Yale University Press.

7. "Logan and Lincoln," by William H. Townsend, American Bar Ass'n Journal, Vol. XIX, No. 2 (February, 1933) pp. 87-93.

8. Abraham Lincoln's Prairie Years, by Carl Sandburg, Vol. I, Chap. 60, p. 293.

CHAPTER 2

ANIMAL TRIALS

"If the law supposes that," said Mr. Bumble, "the law is an ass, an idiot."
— Oliver Twist, by Charles Dickens

ALMOST every animal and insect has had its day in court. During the Middle Ages animal trials were very popular. A reliable authority lists over two hundred such trials in a single century.[1]

Gaspard Bailly of Chambery, France, published a book devoted solely to animal trials, containing forms of indictments, modes of pleading and all manner of legal technicalities to be invoked by way of defense. His work was well received by lawyers even as late as 1688 and became a ready reference of the courts which conducted such trials.

Ecclesiastical rather than civil courts assumed jurisdiction of most cases involving insects and rodents. The reason was that bishop-courts could do what law-courts could not do, namely, place a curse of the church on them. Usually after several insects were tried, convicted and solemnly put to death, their associates were "excommunicated."

Freak trials involving dumb animals as "murder suspects" were solemnly conducted by the judiciary of most European countries up to the last century. Oftentimes such brutal proceedings were just sadistic spectacles, furnishing an "eyeful" to the vast multitude of onlookers who loudly huzzahed when the death sentence was pronounced.

THE TRIAL OF THE WEEVILS

A legal historian by the name of M. Leon Menebrea[2] devoted over twenty-eight pages to the trial of some weevils and declared in 1906 that the original court records (compiled in 1587) were still intact in the archives of St. Julien.

Because of the damage done by weevils to many vineyards near St. Julien, France, in 1545, legal indictments were drawn and the insects were actually defended in court. On May 8, 1546, a proclamation was issued, and, curiously enough, the bothersome weevils disappeared, their descendants returning, however, in 1587. They were again criminally indicted, the trial ending December 20th of that year, without any known decision except that the insects were given some acreage in fee simple.[3]

THE TRIAL OF THE ANTS

In 1713, the ants in Pridade no Maranhao, Brazil, were charged with undermining cellars and carrying off flour from stores. They were represented by counsel, who argued at length before a church court sitting in the monastery of Saint Anthony. A verdict was returned against the ants, and sentence was actually proclaimed aloud by one of the friars who, pursuant to order of court, went out to the ant-hills.[4]

THE TRIAL OF THE MOSQUITOES

During the thirteenth century, some mosquitoes were criminally indicted by the people of Mayenee. When they failed to appear in answer to the summons, the court appointed a lawyer to act on their behalf. So well did counsel plead their cause that the court took pity, and, in banishing them, transferred certain real estate outside of Mayenee "to be for their use and behoof forever."[5]

TRIALS OF CATERPILLARS, LOCUSTS, FLIES AND CRICKETS

Caterpillars have stood trial during many centuries. In 866 they were criminally indicted in Roman Campagna. Six hundred years later, caterpillars were tried before a law court in Macon. In 1584 they were excommunicated by the Grand Vicar of Valence, who cited the insects to appear before him and proceeded to appoint a proctor to defend them. History reveals that their cause was solemnly argued and that they were sentenced to quit the diocese. However, as they failed to obey the order of the court, the grotesque trial continued until most of the caterpillars (who are short-

29

lived) died off. The Vicar was then credited with having miraculously exterminated them.

The last known trial involving locusts as defendants took place in Clemont Ferrand in 1829. A French historian by the name of Desmoyer gives a detailed account of the proceeding in his unique book entitled *Recherches*.[6]

During the Middle Ages, actions were instigated against even flies and crickets.[7]

EELS' RIGHTS

Between 1221 and 1229, Guillaume de Saluces, Bishop of Lausanne, conducted an ecclesiastical hearing involving the light of certain eels to occupy Lake Lemon. After a lengthy trial in which many lawyers participated, the court enjoined the eels from occupying all but a certain designated portion of the lake. A full report of the lawsuit was related by a celebrated Zurich lawyer named Felix Malleobus who died in 1457.[8]

EXCOMMUNICATION OF DOVES

A bizarre performance took place in Canada during the latter part of the seventeenth century. Doves were made the subject of prosecution and, after solemn trial, wherein witnesses testified and authorities were quoted, were excommunicated by decree of the Bishop of Montreal for the damage they had done.[9]

LEECHES BROUGHT TO JUSTICE

A number of leeches were brought into an ecclesiastical court in 1451 in Lausanne. They were forced to "hear" the reading of a document which admonished them to leave the district within three days. When they proved incorrigible, the bishop-court exorcised them for not having left the country.[10]

In medieval days, many people believed that animals might either be possessed of the Devil or be the Devil himself and, as such, had no right to live; but they were willing to accord the unfortunates proper legal defense and ceremony before execution. No rational explanation has ever been advanced for these fantastic performances. However, these farces of the law have been recorded by so many legal historians that there is no reason to doubt their authenticity; and grotesque as the ceremonies were, they never failed to draw an audience in those days when entertainment was scarce. From the very time moles were tried in Western Tyrol (Commune of Stelvio) by juries in the ninth century,[11] to more recent days when dogs have been put on trial, crowds have made a festival of such occasions.

In 1479, the inhabitants of Lausanne petitioned the Chancellor of Berne to rid the community of grasshoppers. Technically treated as defendants, the insects were assigned the services of a lawyer already dead, and actually cited to appear in the Bishop's court at Berne, Switzerland. Upon their failure to appear, the grasshoppers were excommunicated and their descendants were ordered "to quit forever the diocese of Lausanne."[12]

THE ROOSTER SORCERER

Absurd as it may seem, authentic sources reveal that a rooster was tried before a court sitting in Basle, Switzerland, in 1474—accused of being a sorcerer! The prosecutor contended that this rooster aided witchcraft inasmuch as it had laid eggs. It was shown that most sorcerers would rather possess a cock's egg than a philosopher's stone, and that Satan employed witches to hatch such eggs, from which proceeded winged serpents most dangerous to mankind.

On behalf of the rooster-prisoner, the facts of the case were admitted, but his advocate submitted that no evil animus had been proved against his client and that no injury to man or beast had resulted. It was also contended that the laying of an egg was an involuntary act; and, as such, not punishable by law.

The Court refused to follow the argument advanced by the rooster's attorney, and convicted the unfortunate fowl of sorcery. Both the rooster and the egg which it had allegedly laid were burned at the stake "with all of the required form and solemnity of a judicial execution."[13]

Roosters have acted as court attachés as well as accused criminals. Only the crow of a rooster adjourned the "Lawless Court" of Essex, England, for more than three hundred years. At midnight of the Wednesday following old Michaelmas

Day of every year until 1790, the "Lawless Court" convened at the outskirts of Rothford, near Southend on King's Hill in the County of Essex. It was a manorial court and by custom heard petty collection cases, together with eviction and rent-arrearage matters, relating to the lord's manor. Court session did not legally end, however, until a rooster's shrill chanticleer was heard at daybreak.[14]

It is also an established fact that chickens have served as prosecutors; for even to the present day, when someone has been murdered on the Islands of Nias in the Pacific, the suspects form a circle and a chicken actually chooses the murderer. All those accused of the crime are forced to gather around in a ring, into which a fowl is thrown, and the one against whose leg the chicken runs is proclaimed guilty.[15]

PIGS ON TRIAL

The famous historian, Ab. Ruchat, recorded this strange trial. He said: "In 1364 the church of Chattens, in the Jorat Hills, the range of which Lausanne is the capital, possessed

a miraculous image of St. Pancrace. A pig having destroyed a child, the aforesaid image was brought out, and the child was restored to life. The pig was then cited for murder and caused to appear in the Bishop's Court at Lausanne and found guilty of wilful murder and sentenced to death."[16]

In Falaise, France, 1386, a pig was sentenced to be executed in man's clothing. It was actually tried in court for murdering an infant by trampling it to death. The entire populace turned out to witness the bizarre spectacle. Amid the huzzahs of the crowd, the pig was condemned to die by hanging on the public gibbet. It was ordered by the court to be dressed in human clothes, and, after being unmercifully whipped and maimed, was hanged.[17]

An entire herd of swine was arrested September 5, 1370, because three of its number had killed the son of a swineherd. The Duke of Burgundy, sitting as a court, was impressed with the plea advanced by the owner of the swine and ordered only the three sows to be executed, "notwithstanding that the others had seen the death of the boy without defending him."

Nine years later, two entire herds of swine were sentenced to death by Philip the Bold for being accomplices to an infanticide in Saint Marcel-lez-Jussey, France. On September 12, 1379, letters patent were issued and through the intervention of a friar named Humbert de Poutiers, the culprits were pardoned.[18]

RATS UP FOR BURGLARY

In 1510, rats were charged with burglary in the province of Autun, France. The "dirty animals" (as they were described in the citations) were indicted for having wantonly destroyed the barley crop. The court appointed a young lawyer named Bartholomew de Chassenée to defend them. When the rats failed to appear, Chassenée successfully argued that only a few defendants had been cited and, as the case involved all the rats of the diocese, all of them should be summoned. Again the rats failed to appear, whereupon the French advo-

35

cate contended that his clients were afraid to come because of "evilly disposed cats" which were in constant watch along the highways; and since the accused were entitled to protection to and from court, the plaintiff should post a bond to be forfeited in the event the cats attacked the rats on their way to court.[19]

The record is incomplete, so the verdict is unknown. Chassenée, however, established an enviable legal reputation on account of the case and has since been regarded by many historians as one of the greatest lawyers France has ever produced.[20] He later produced a treatise in which he established the principle that animals could be proper parties for excommunication and anathema; and that if they failed to obey clerical authorities, they could be lawfully turned over to the civil authorities for capital punishment. Thus, no being was immune from the grasp of the law.

Whenever a pestilence swept a community and the townspeople believed there were too many mice or rats, legal complaints were drawn and filed in court. The animals under indictment would then be summoned to appear on a certain day, and if they did not appear judgment would be entered against them by default. But the judiciary of days gone by were sticklers for granting due process of law and prided themselves on being eminently fair, so that when someone urged a legal defense the whole town turned out to hear it.

In many of these animal trials, testimony was introduced tending to prove that, as the accused were possessed by demons, their crimes had been premeditated. As black was thought to be Satan's color, animals bearing the color were supposedly disguised as the Devil. Black cats were severely prejudiced for this reason when brought to trial.

A BULL MURDERER

In 1313, at Moisy, France, a bull was charged with murder, having gored a man so badly that he died. The court convicted the animal and ordered death on the gibbet. The decision was appealed to Parliament which ruled that, although the indictment and conviction were legal, the trial court was without jurisdiction. During the appeal the bull was imprisoned along with the human prisoners, as was the general custom in such trials.[21]

A BEAR JURY?

In 1499, a bear which had ravaged Schwarzwald villages came up for trial, ably defended by a lawyer who insisted upon a trial by a jury of the bear's peers. A delay of more than a week was obtained because of argument on this technicality. [22]

CONVICTIONS OF COWS

In 1546, the Parliament of Paris, France, considered with all seriousness a criminal case which involved the issue whether a cow could be legally guilty of murder. Many subcommittee reports were drafted and presented. The animal itself was brought in for review before the assembly's provost. After much discord and wrangle, the unfortunate beast was deemed a proper subject of conviction; so the earlier conviction was let stand. Sixty-three years later another cow was convicted by the Parliament of Paris.[23]

A donkey was tried in 1768 at Nismes, in Languedoc, for the crime of sacrilege. It was shown that the animal had drunk holy water from a basin in a church. The accused was represented by counsel who argued at length but to no avail. Sentence was passed and the donkey was hanged on the gibbet. The costs were borne by its owner, a gardener.[24]

PROSECUTED HORSES

French annals of jurisprudence cite several instances where horses were made the subject of criminal prosecution. The court of Dijon twice condemned and executed horses for homicide—once in 1389 and again in 1639.

A mare was burned to death in Aix as late as 1694 by order of the highest judicial tribunal of the province.[20]

Fighting roosters have been heralded in court many times to answer criminal charges, usually that of cock-fighting.

The latest case of this kind took place in 1938 in the Court of Special Sessions in New York City. Forty-six men were awaiting sentence on their pleas of guilty to "witnessing an animal fight." The evidence consisted of an expert on the subject of cock-fighting and the four roosters who participated

in the affray. Each fowl had been carried into the courtroom in a separate wooden crate, midst a crowd of several hundred spectators.

The courtroom soon turned into a bedlam as the cocks began to crow and flap their wings. Despite this handicap, the defense counsel ably stressed his plea for leniency. To cap the climax, one of the "evidence" flew up on the bench in front of the judge and perched himself on a law book which contained the legal definition of what constituted cock-fighting. Soon the court pronounced sentence of guilty, with the cocks still crowing, and the spectators still holding their sides laughing.

Some years ago it was against the law in South Bend for anyone to smoke a cigarette in public. A showman allowed his chimpanzee to smoke before an amused crowd in violation of the ordinance. As a result the animal was hailed into court and after a full hearing was convicted and fined.[25]

RECENT ANIMAL CONVICTIONS

A foxhound was convicted by a jury in 1925 for killing sheep at Winchester, Kentucky.[26]

In 1927, the Circuit Court of Frederick County, Virginia, imposed a death sentence upon a dog charged with sheep-murder.[27]

So the bringing of dumb animals to the bar of justice is not a thing solely confined to the past. In 1932, a German police dog was solemnly tried in Richmond, Virginia, and upon conviction was sentenced to life imprisonment in the Henrico County jail.[28]

As recently as 1933 four dogs were legally tried in McGraw, New York, for biting six-year-old Joyce Hammond. A lawyer even appeared on behalf of one of the dogs. After a full hearing before an audience of one hundred and fifty people, the dogs were convicted and subsequently executed. In pronouncing the death sentence, Justice A. P. McGraw said:

"A great responsibility rests on one who has to decide in the place of a jury. I have great sympathy for dogs and their owners. I know the value of a good dog. But this is a serious case. Something must be done to guard against such things in the future. The dogs are criminals of the worst kind. I order them placed under observation for rabies until February 15, 1933, when they will be killed by the county veterinarian."

In Baldwinsville, New York, a dog wearing chains was put on trial for its life because it bit a boy in the back.

At Hudson Falls, New York, a four-year probation was recently given a Spitz dog which was charged with biting a woman. The same year a black spaniel convicted in Jersey City of murdering a child was granted four different reprieves from the death-chamber.

A few years ago a six-month-old puppy named Idaho was indicted in Brockport, New York, for having caused a fourteen-year-old boy to drown. After the State rested its case, came an army of defense witnesses, some to establish character and some to establish an alibi. After the lawyers pleaded mistaken identity and appealed at great length for mercy, the court ordered the dog's life saved and put the animal on probation for two years.

Thus, despite the present-day tendency to hold the owner alone responsible, there are instances even of recent date where dumb animals have been brought to trial and actually sentenced for their own alleged crimes. The couplet found in *Drunken Barnaby's Four Journeys* concerning the "hanging of his cat on Monday, for killing of a mouse on Sunday" is no idle witticism!

SOURCES

Chapter 2

1. Credulities, Past and Present (1880), by William Jones, F.S.A., footnote, p. 300.

2. Jugements Renders Leon Contre les Animaux, by M. Menebrea (1846), pp. 546, et seq.

3. Memoires de la Société Royale Academique de Savoie, Tome XII, pp. 524-557.

4. Curiosites Judiciares et Historique, by M. Emile Aguel.

5. Curiosities of Olden Times, by S. Baring-Gould, p. 66.

6. Curiosities of Law and Lawyers, by Croake James, p. 143.

7. Memoires de la Société Royale Academique de Savoie.

8. Credulities, Past and Present (1880), by William Jones, F.S.A., p. 296.

9. Noveaux Voyages dans l'Amerique Septentribual, by Baron de la Hautan.

10. Memoires de la Société des Antiquaires (1829), by M. Berriat Saint Prix.

11. Animal Prisoner at the Bar, by J. P. McNamara, The Notre Dame Lawyer, Vol. III, No. 1, pp. 30, 36.

12. History of the Swiss Reformation, by Ab. Ruchat.

13. Curiosities of Law & Lawyers, by William Andrews, p. 160.

14. The Lawless Court of Essex, by Courtney Kenny, 5 Columbia Law Review (7), pp. 529-536.

15. The Islands of Nias—at the Edge of the World, by M. C. Cole.

16. History of the Swiss Reformation, by Ab. Ruchat.

17. L'Annuaire de l'Aisne (1812), by M. Boileau de Maulaville, p. 88.

18. Revue des Sociétés Savantes (1866), by M. Garnier, p. 476.

19. Curiosities of Law and Lawyers, by William Andrews, p. 160.

20. Trials of Animals, by Thomas Frost, p. 151.

21. Criminal Prosecution and Capital Punishment of Animals, pp. 160, 161.

22. Medieval Animal Trials, by A. Alexander.

23. Siècle de Louis XIV, Chap. 1, by Voltaire.

24. Curiosities of Law and Lawyers, by Croake James, p. 658.

25. The Notre Dame Lawyer, Vol. III, No. 1, p. 36.

26. The Lawyer, June, 1938, p. 20.

27. The Notre Dame Lawyer, Vol. III, No. 1, p. 36.

28. Henrico County Records (1932), Richmond, Virginia.

CHAPTER 3

POSTHUMOUS TRIALS

"As literature, the law is full of dead men's bones."
—Arthur Train

SOME of the most celebrated people in history have had the most unusual court experiences. Many of them have been tried after death.

POPE FORMOSUS

The earliest recorded case involving a posthumous trial was that of Pope Formosus. It took place in 896 in Rome and has been regarded by many as one of the strangest proceedings in the annals of jurisprudence.

Pope Formosus had crowned Arnulf Emperor of the Roman Empire and by so doing had incurred the enmity of the mother of Arnulf's rival, so that when Formosus died, his successor, Pope Stephen VI, was prevailed upon to conduct a macabre ceremony.

An indictment, in accordance with the law of the times, was drawn up charging the late Pope with usurpation of the papal throne which he had occupied for five years. The corpse, which had been in the tomb only eight months, was withdrawn; and, being clad in papal arrayment, was propped up on the witness chair located in the throne room. A synod composed of many papal dignitaries assembled. In order to comply properly with the laws of the living, the accused was legally represented by a deacon who had been appointed by the synod to defend.

Pope Stephen headed the court which sat in judgment upon the remains of their former papal leader. After a lengthy

trial, which was conducted strictly along legal lines, the decedent was adjudged guilty. Sentence was passed declaring his pontificate invalid and annuling all his acts and measures. The court attachés then stripped the corpse of its papal cloth and threw it in the Tiber River. Later, the sentence was set aside by one of Stephen's successors and the memory of Formosus was, in law, vindicated and restored.[1]

THOMAS A BECKET

Another important posthumous trial was that of Thomas à Becket, the great Archbishop of Canterbury, who was tried more than 350 years after his death. He was murdered in 1170

at the age of fifty-three. Lord Campbell in his *Lives of the Lord Chancellors* said:

"The [English] government tried to palliate and justify the murder. The archbishop of York likened Thomas à Becket to Pharoah, who died by the Divine vengeance as a punishment for his hardness of heart; and a proclamation was issued forbidding anyone to speak of Thomas of Canterbury as a martyr; but the feelings of men were too strong to be checked by authority; pieces of linen which had been dipped in his blood were preserved as relics; from the time of his death it was believed that miracles were worked at his tomb; thither flocked hundreds of thousands, in spite of the most violent threats of punishment; at the end of three years, he was canonized at Rome, and, till the breaking out of the Reformation, St. Thomas of Canterbury, for pilgrimages and prayers, was the most distinguished Saint in England."

Over three hundred and fifty years elapsed and then King Henry VIII summoned the skeleton of Thomas à Becket to appear before the Star Chamber of England. He accused the former Archbishop of usurpation of the papal throne and convicted him after a long-drawn-out trial. Lord Campbell's description of the proceedings is most authentic and reads as follows:

"Henry VIII, when he wished to throw off the authority of the Pope, thinking that as long as the name of St. Thomas should remain in the calendar men would be stimulated by his example to brave the ecclesiastical authority of the Sovereign, instructed his Attorney General to file a quo warranto information against him for usurping the office of a Saint, and he was formally cited to appear in court to answer the charge. Judgment of ouster would have passed against him by default had not the King, to show him impartiality and great regard for the due administration of justice, assigned him counsel at public expense. The cause being called, and the Attorney General and the advocate being fully heard, with such proofs as were offered on both sides, sentence was pronounced, that 'Thomas, sometime Archbishop of Canterbury, had been guilty of contumacy, treason and rebellion; that his bones should be publicly burnt to admonish the living of their duty by the punishment of the dead; and that the offerings made at his shrine should be forfeited to the Crown.' A proclamation followed, stating that 'forasmuch as it now clearly appeared that Thomas à Becket had been killed in a riot excited by his own obstinacy and intemperate language, and had been afterwards canonized by the Bishop of Rome as the champion of his usurped authority, the King's Majesty thought it expedient to declare to his loving subjects that he was no saint, but rather a rebel and traitor to his Prince, and therefore strictly charged and commanded that he should not be esteemed or called a saint; that all images and pictures of him should be destroyed, the festivals in his honor be abolished and his name and remembrance be erased out of all books, under pain of his Majestry's indignation and imprisonment at his Grace's pleasure.' "

Henry the Eighth's disgraceful conduct was erased by a later English ruler who reinstated the good name and title to the memory of the ill-fated Thomas à Becket.[2]

SOURCES

Chapter 3

1. The Lives of the Popes in the Middle Ages, by Rev. H. K. Mann, pp. 81, 82, 93.

2. Lives of the Lord Chancellors, by Lord Campbell, Vol. I, pp. 110, 111.

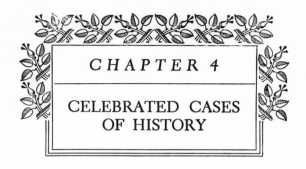

"Lawsuits are frequently ended without having deter-
mined anything except, possibly, the costs."
—Van Arsdale v. King, 155 N. Y. 325 at 329

SOME of the most celebrated lawsuits have centered around inconsequential objects. A strand of hair supposedly belonging to the Prophet Mohammed formed the basis of a famous English case sixty years ago. It was known as the Trial of the Prophet's Beard and caused a real sensation among Mohammedans at Madras. An eccentric Englishman left a substantial amount for ceremonies connected with a sacred relic, known as the "Aussaree Shareef," which was a box containing a hair from the beard of the Prophet. Six different persons claimed ownership of the relic. After a lengthy trial, his Lordship, Mr. Justice Innes, finally disposed of the case in August of 1879. This is the only case on record where a hair was made the subject of dispute.[1]

THE EGYPTIAN MUMMY CASE

An Egyptian mummy was the center of a great judicial combat in an Albany, N. Y., Circuit Court in 1829. It had been stolen while on exhibition in a near-by town and a jury was asked to determine its value. The defense urged that the title to the mummy was in its last lineal descendant and not in the exhibitor. Apparently the jury did not agree; it returned a verdict for $1200 and costs.[2]

DISPUTED IDENTITY

One of the queerest cases in French law records is that of Louis de la Pivardiere of Narbonne, who for over two years endeavored to establish his identity. He had two separate trials, and over two hundred witnesses testified concerning who he was. Even then it took him from August 18, 1697, to June 14, 1701, before he was able to convince the court that he was himself.[3]

ROULETTE WINNINGS

Another unusual French case involved one Labon, who sat down at a roulette table in a gambling casino at Nice and laid, on number 17, counters valued at a thousand francs. His number won, and 35,000 francs were shoved his way. He played the number again and won. His stack remained on the same number, which continued to be successful until over a half-million francs accumulated. Then it was discovered that M. Labon was dead. The owners of the gambling resort decided, however, that the play was regular only for the first turn and refused to give the decedent credit for more than 35,000 francs. Suit was filed by M. Labon's widow, who claimed her late husband's estate was entitled to the entire fortune of a half-million francs.[4] Just what decision the French court reached is not known.

THE TICHBORNE IMPOSTORS

The most remarkable case involving disputed identity—as well as the longest criminal case ever recorded in England—

was tried in 1874 before the Court of Queen's Bench in Westminster Hall, London. Twenty years before, Sir Roger Tichborne, the younger, had left England for South America and was reported drowned off the coast of Brazil. In 1866, Arthur (Bull) Orton, of Wagga Wagga, Australia, appeared in London claiming to be the long-lost Tichborne. The mistake the claimant made upon arrival was to look up the Orton family in Wapping Wharf before going to the Tichborne home. This caused Scotland Yard to put Inspector

William Denning, a famous detective, on the trace of Bull Orton's antecedents and former activities as an Australian bushranger, outlaw and butcher. Lady Tichborne, the mother of the lost heir, identified Orton as her son because of the marked resemblance he bore to her young Roger; the rest of the Tichborne family refused to accept him. Orton instituted a civil suit for recovery of the valuable Tichborne estates. One hundred and twenty-one witnesses entered the box and declared the claimant was no impostor, but the missing heir. In the midst of the civil trial, the wanderer from Australia chose to have his case dismissed after learning that the jury did not favor his cause. Thereupon, the Lord Chief Justice committed Orton to Newgate Prison. On April 23, 1873, Arthur Orton, alias Thomas Castre, alias Sir Roger Charles Tichborne, stood up and pleaded not guilty to an indictment covering several hundred feet of parchment which charged him with wilful and corrupt perjury. Defended by Dr. Edward V. Kenealy, who honestly believed his client to be the real heir, Orton conveniently forgot his past and spent thirty-four days in the witness box in an effort to convince a jury of his peers that he was no impostor. The Crown put on 215 witnesses, many of whom came from South America, the United States and Australia, but the defense introduced a similar number of witnesses. On February 28, 1874, the one hundred and eighty-eighth day of the trial, the case went to the jury, which returned a verdict of guilty within a half hour.

Orton was sentenced to fourteen years of hard labor, but was released ten years later for good behavior. His lawyer was disbarred but later became a member of Parliament. In 1898

Orton died in Marylebone, England, in complete poverty and obscurity. To the very end he contended that he was no impostor; on his coffin he had inscribed the name of Sir Roger Charles Tichborne.[5]

In 1904, a second claimant appeared. He was William Cresswell, an inmate of an Australian asylum who claimed he should be released for the reason that he was the real Tichborne. The court denied relief, but found that Cresswell undisputably "had in his possession papers and effects belonging to the real Tichborne"; and that the missing heir had not drowned but was rescued and reached Australia, where, before he died in Melbourne, in 1860, he fell in with Orton and Cresswell.[6]

ROPE JUSTICE

The weird case of Will Purvis, native of Marion County, Mississippi, is another curious story. Purvis was charged with murdering a man who had testified before a grand jury against the Ku Klux Klan, of which Purvis was a member. The State's key witness was the brother of the murdered man. He related that he had been with the decedent at the time the crime was committed and was positive in identifying Purvis as the trigger man. Although Purvis was ably defended by a former state senator, the jury returned a verdict of guilty, and he was sentenced on August 5, 1893. He was "strung up" before five thousand Mississippians; but the rope, being cut flush with the knot, slipped, and Purvis fell to the ground unhurt. When the executioner was about to hang him again, the crowd opposed it, shouting: "He's been hung one too many times, already!" The convicted man was led back to jail. However,

53

the Supreme Court of Mississippi held that the sentence of hanging would have to be carried out again. The public became aroused the day before the day set for the execution, and Purvis' friends helped him escape until after the gubernatorial election, which involved the issue whether or not Purvis should be hanged, if caught. As the candidate favoring the life sentence was elected, Purvis voluntarily returned and spent time in prison. On December 19, 1898, he was pardoned—after the murdered man's brother withdrew his testimony of identification.

Nineteen years later, the real murderer confessed to the crime on his death-bed. Thus, "by a twist of fate and the slip of a rope," says Professor Borchard in his *Convicting the Innocent*, an innocent man's life was saved. In 1920, almost twenty-five years later, the legislature of Mississippi appropriated $5,000 to farmer Will Purvis (then forty-six years old) as compensation "for the services done and performed . . . in the State Penitentiary under the provision of an erroneous judgment."[7]

CAPTAIN KIDD'S EXECUTION

The trial of Captain Kidd, the notorious pirate, is not to be omitted in the field of strange decisions. It was his case that established the precedent that one can legally be hanged twice. In 1701 Kidd was charged with piracy and forced to stand trial in the famous London criminal court, Old Bailey. Conviction quickly followed the trial and the world-famous pirate, then fifty-six years old, was sent across the river to Wapping Wharf for execution. The halter and scaffold broke the first time he was strung up. He was found to be still alive; so the question arose whether he could be hanged again. After reflection the court ruled that he could be, and a few minutes later the execution was renewed and the activities of the Captain were put to an end.[8]

THE DRED SCOTT DECISION

Many historians have said that no legal controversy in the United States has equaled the Dred Scott case in point of historic importance.

In 1834, an army surgeon by the name of Dr. John Emerson took his slave, Dred Scott, out of Missouri to Fort Snelling in the Wisconsin Territory, then free by the Missouri Compromise. Four years later the doctor returned to his home in St. Louis and brought Scott with him. Six years later Emerson died and willed his property to his wife in trust for his daughter. Mrs. Emerson did not want to own any slaves, but her right to emancipate was questionable under the terms of her husband's will. When Mrs. Emerson moved from Missouri to Massachusetts she failed to take Dred Scott with her.

Eventually, the slave became a charge on a previous master, Taylor Blow, who suggested to Messrs. Field & Hall, a well-known legal firm in St. Louis, that they come to Scott's aid and test out the law on slavery. Should the courts declare that Scott had been illegally held as a slave since his trip with his master to a free territory, a successful suit would lie against the Emerson estate for his twelve years' wages.

Hence, during the fall of 1846, Dred Scott signed his cross to a petition which was filed in the Missouri State Court, claiming damages for technical false imprisonment and assault and battery against his mistress, Irene Emerson. ". . . it was this action, undoubtedly instigated by attorneys with mercenary motives, that led the way to a cause célèbre, destined to make history and to prove one of the provocations of the Civil War." (Page 118, *Decisive Battles of the Law*, by Frederick Trevor Hill. New York, 1907. Harper & Bros.)

After the case had been in the state courts some eight years, the Supreme Court of Missouri decided against Scott. (11 Mo. Rep. 413 and 15 Mo. Rep. 557.)

In the meantime, Mrs. Emerson transferred her ownership of Scott to her brother, John Sanford, who was a resident of New York. On the ground of diversity of citizenship, Scott filed suit in the Federal Circuit Court for the District of Missouri (No. 692, November 2, 1853), claiming $9,000 damages for assault and imprisonment. Since the story that Scott was beaten by his master had no real foundation in fact, this claim was more nominal than real. The local Federal Judge held that Scott and his family were the lawful property of the defendant, Sanford.

The case was then appealed to the United States Supreme Court on May 15, 1854. Dred Scott's lawyer began searching for legal assistance. To Montgomery Blair in Washington he wrote as follows:

"A year ago I was employed to bring a suit in favor of one Dred Scott, a black man held in slavery. . . . The question involved is the much-vexed one whether the removal by the master of his slave to Illinois or Wisconsin works an absolute emancipation. . . . If you or any other gentleman at Washington should feel interest enough in the case to give it such attention as to bring it to a hearing and decision by the Court, the cause of humanity may perhaps be subserved; at all events a much-disputed question would be settled by the highest court of the nation."

More than a year passed after this letter was written before the case was argued, but, in the meantime, it had not been forgotten by the politicians. On March 6, 1857, a decision was reached. The Court held (7 to 2) that Scott was not a citizen and not entitled to any standing in court. Chief Justice Taney wrote that a negro had "no rights which a white man was bound to respect."[9]

Thousands of copies of the opinion were printed and disseminated over the entire country. Mass meetings and northern newspapers vigorously attacked the decision and within a short while Dred Scott became a national character.

Neither Sanford nor Dred Scott lived to see the war that followed their great legal battle. Scott died in St. Louis on September 17, 1858, a victim of consumption.

A strange case, recently decided, involved the man who sued his doctor because he did not die. Dr. Benjafield, of Hobart, Tasmania, gave E. J. Ison, of Mangalere, only five months to live. The patient, relying upon the doctor's statement, sold his business at a sacrifice and closed his affairs. He waited for death, but through some miracle recovered. Suit was subsequently filed for damages sustained by reason of continuing to live. Incidentally, the patient outlived the doctor.[10]

THE DUTCH NATION INDICTED

The historian Jean François le Petit refers to the celebrated Dutch case of the sixteenth century where the three million people of the Netherlands were indicted as a nation and convicted of the crime of heresy and sentenced to death. By decree of the Holy Office of the Inquisition in Madrid, dated February 19, 1568, all of the people of Holland were found guilty of heresy, apostasy and defection, and sentenced seven days later, by virtue of the death warrant which King Philip II signed. All of this came about soon after the accession of Philip, who invoked a policy of severe and relentless religious persecution which caused his Dutch subjects to rebel. The original death warrant signed by the king is now in the Escorial in Spain.[11]

CHRISTOPHER COLUMBUS' TRIAL

Christopher Columbus was legally enjoined by a Haiti court from "ever setting foot again on the soil of the New

World." History records that on March 21, 1499, King Ferdinand of Spain ordered Commander Francisco de Bobadilla to proceed to Santo Domingo and try Columbus for the crime of excessive cruelty to natives. Bobadilla arrived in Haiti in October, and immediately summoned Columbus to trial. Columbus was found guilty and forthwith sentenced to be deported to Spain in chains. By virtue of this court decree, Columbus lost all his rights and privileges and was by law prohibited from returning to this continent.[12]

THE BIDWELL GANG IN LONDON

In 1872, the Bidwell gang came to London from the United States. They gained the confidence of local tradesmen who introduced them to officials of the Bank of England. Thereafter, they forged the names of local concerns on bills of exchange not due for ninety days. During the three-month interim, these daring criminals received from the bank over £100,000. Finally, a missing date on a forged draft led a bank clerk to approach one of the alleged makers, and the Bidwell brothers were sentenced to penal servitude for life.[13]

GALILEO'S PERJURY

Galileo was another famous person who encountered the courts in a most unusual way. It was in June of 1633 that the great astronomer was by law forced to commit perjury in order to save his own life. Because he taught that the earth moved around the sun, he was sentenced to recount the seven penitential psalms once a week for a period of three years.[14]

JOAN OF ARC AS LAWYER

About five hundred years ago, Jeanne d'Arc was arraigned before some sixty judges to answer charges of heresy. The courtroom was crowded, but those who managed to get in witnessed the Maid serve as her own lawyer; and, judging from the record, she defended herself better than any lawyer could ever have hoped to do. As everyone knows, the judges were only hirelings of the English, and consequently she was doomed to death.[15]

A SEVEN-YEAR TRIAL

Warren Hastings, first Governor General of British India, also occupies a unique position in this field of strange cases. He was charged with robbery, bribery and embezzlement. He was impeached and stood trial for over seven years. His trial began in Westminster Hall, on February 13, 1788, and did not end until April 23, 1795. During this famous proceeding, sixty peers died and the Lord Chancellor resigned. Over a half-million dollars was expended by both sides before Hastings was finally acquitted.[16]

Socrates was seventy years old when he tangled with the law. The venerable philosopher was charged with corrupting the youth of Athens by introducing new divinities. Formal accusation was lodged against him in 399 B.C., and the trial took place before a dikastery or law court. Five hundred and one persons made up the jury which voted him the death penalty. In ancient days it was not uncommon for juries to number as high as one thousand.[17]

THE HAYMARKET SQUARE CASE

A most peculiar case took place in Chicago in the summer of 1886. It was known as the Haymarket Square case. Eight anarchists were up for first-degree murder.

A mass meeting had been held near Haymarket Square on the night of May 4, 1886. The crowd had gathered to protest against the action of police in suppressing disorder during a widespread strike to enforce the eight-hour day. While the meeting was still in session a company of police appeared and ordered the crowd to disburse. Someone hurled a bomb which killed seven policemen and wounded sixty others. The assassin escaped, but within a week almost every well-known anarchist in Chicago was placed under arrest. The newspapers carried front-page stories of the wholesale murder and public feeling ran high. Honorable Joseph E. Gary presided.

There was such widespread public prejudice that twenty-two days of ceaseless examination of potential jurors were required (during which time no less than 981 persons were examined) before enough jurors could be found who were held to be sufficiently unprejudiced to be sworn. After almost two months of trial, the jury retired, and a few hours later brought in a verdict of guilty.

But the case was still far from settled. Seven of the defendants were sentenced to hang and one to fifteen years' imprisonment. Subsequently, one committed suicide. The sentences of two of the remaining six were commuted to life imprisonment; so finally four were hanged. The case went to the Illinois Supreme Court and the United States Supreme Court and, in addition, there were hearings before the Governor of Illinois.[18]

THE LONGEST CIVIL CASE

The longest civil case ever tried in the United States was the "Willett-Sears" case, tried in 1924, in Norfolk County, Massachusetts.[19]

On March 10, 1927, a full Bench of the Massachusetts Supreme Court set aside the verdict and found in favor of the defendants, ruling that the release which the plaintiffs gave the defendants served as a complete defense. Some time later the United States Supreme Court declined to review the controversy, thereby putting an end to the longest case ever submitted to an American judge and jury.

In 1918, George F. Willett and his partner, Edmund H. Sears, borrowed $3,000,000 from various Boston banks and transferred stock which they had in various companies in order to secure the loan. Sometime thereafter, Mr. Willett charged several banking firms with conspiring to ruin his credit. In the bill of complaint, Willett alleged that fraud and duress had been practiced upon him and that the general release which he had executed for $125,000 could not stand. He contended that the defendants had misrepresented the financial status of certain companies, saying that they were on the eve of bankruptcy, and for that reason he had surrendered his rights to certain stocks.

The trial began on November 8, 1923, before Judge Christopher T. Callahan and a jury in the Norfolk County Superior Court at Dedham. Sherman L. Whipple and Boyd B. Jones served as counsel for Mr. Willett, and George L. Mayberry, Hugh D. McLellan and Thomas Hunt acted as chief counsel for the defense. The hearing continued for thirteen months and did not end until December 18, 1924. On that date the jury returned its verdict in favor of Mr. Willett in the sum of $10,534,109.07. It has been understood that Mr. Willett first tried to get the Honorable Charles E. Hughes, former Secretary of State and then Chief Justice of the United States Supreme Court, to serve as his counsel.

Length of proceedings—184 actual trial days.
Damages claimed—15 million dollars.

Jury awarded $10,534,109.07, but Supreme Court of Massachusetts allowed nothing.

Words spoken by witnesses and lawyers were over 4 million.

One witness on stand 55 days.

Cost of trial to Norfolk County—$35,000.

Jurors were paid $19,656 (for salaries and mileage).

As one juror collapsed by reason of nervous disorder during trial in 1924, the case was finished in trial court with only *eleven* jurors.

During the trial two of the jurors were married.

Judge Christopher T. Callahan, presiding judge, had an attack of angina pectoris during the trial.

Twelve women related to counsel, witnesses, defendant or juror died during the trial.

SOURCES

Chapter 4

1. Ancient, Curious and Famous Wills, by Virgil M. Harris, Little, Brown & Co., pages 184, 185.

2. Pleasantries about Courts and Lawyers, Circuit Court, Albany, N. Y. (1829), p. 29.

3. Judicial Dramas, by Henry Spicer.

4. Ohio Law Reporter.

5. The Trial at Bar of Sir Roger C. D. Tichborne, Vol. I through Vol. VIII, by E. V. Kenealy.

6. Westminster Review, May, 1905.

7. State v. Will Purvis, 71 Miss. Reports (1893) 706-710, Case No. 1036, Marion County Circuit Court (First District). Convicting the Innocent, by Edwin Borchard, Yale University Press.

8. Trial of Captain Kidd, by Graham Brooks.

9. Dred Scott v. Sandford, 13 Howard 393.

10. 29 Illinois Law Review (1934).

11. Chronique, by Jean François le Petit, Vol. 2, p. 174.

12. Life of Columbus, by Justin Winsor.

13. The Bank of England Forgery, by George Dilnot.

14. Great Men and Famous Women, Part 24, Vol. III, 8th Ed., p. 164.

15. The Trial of Jeanne d'Arc, by W. P. Barrett.

16. Famous Trials of History, by Rt. Hon. Birkenhead, p. 161.

17. Historical Trials, by MacDonald.

18. Decisive Battles of the Law, by F. T. Hill, p. 251.
    People v. *Spies et al.*, Criminal Court of Cook County, Illinois, No. 1195 (1886).
    Eagle Forgotten, the Life of John Peter Altgeld, by Harry Barnard.

19. "Willett-Sears" case, 242 Mass. 471.

CHAPTER 5

JUDICIAL HUMOR

*"It is common error to suppose that our law has no
sense of humor because for the most part the judges
who expound it have none."*
—Scintillae Juris, by Mr. Justice Darling

"S OMETIMES judges themselves may be ignorant of
the law."[1] This fact, combined with occasional wit
from judges, keeps instructions to juries from being
devoid of humor.

THE WITTIEST JUDGE

Mr. Justice Darling, Judge of the King's Bench Division at
the turn of this century, has often been called the wittiest
English judge that ever lived.[2]

In his Lordship's court some years ago, counsel became
very diffuse and wasted much time in cross-examining a witness. He had begun by asking the witness how many children
she had, and concluded by asking the same question. Before
the witness could reply, Justice Darling interposed with the
suave remark, "When you began, she had three."

At another time when the qualifications of a singer were at
issue, one of the witnesses said, "Well, he could not sing like
the archangel Gabriel." To which eminent counsel observed

66

that he had never heard the archangel Gabriel. Mr. Justice Darling swiftly rejoined, "That, sir, is a pleasure yet to come."

HOSS SENSE

Judge Squire Sprigg, of Butler County, Ohio, delivered one of the funniest charges ever found. The value of a dead horse was in dispute. At the close of all the evidence, the old judge charged the jury in the following language: [3]

"Gentlemen of the Jury: This is a hoss case. We make quick work of hoss cases in this court. These people killed Doc's old hoss; if Doc's hoss was worth anything, then he is entitled to recovery; if he wasn't worth anything, then he ain't. Some hosses are worth something and a good many more are worth nothing. So, it is for you to say, whether this hoss was worth anything or not. You are to be governed by the preponderance of testimony. Preponderance is a big word, which I must explain to you. It means this: If one side has fifty witnesses and you think they are all liars, and the other side has one witness, and you don't think he is a liar, or at least as big a liar as the other fifty, then the testimony of the one will preponderate over that of the others, and will knock the socks off of the other fifty. Now, if by a preponderance of the testimony, as I have explained it to you, you think the Doc's old hoss was worth anything, find what that is and give it to him; if you think he was worth nothing, why say so. Doc will think this is pretty hard on the medical profession, but he will have to take the medicine which the law prescribes. The law provides for just such cases; it calls this *damnum absque injuria*, which means, as I interpret it, that a man is usually hurt a darned sight less than he thinks he is.

"Now, gentlemen, I believe I have covered the whole case.

You have heard the evidence and the law as I have given it to you. Remember that you are under oath in this business and that the Court expects quick verdicts, especially in hoss cases."

Another humorous charge was delivered in 1911 to a grand jury by a South Carolina judge who said: [4]

"The loss of human life in this country is fearful. I was reading the other day an article published in a reputable periodical, in which it stated that 50,000 people had been killed in this country during the past year, more than enough to make up the standing army of the United States. And out of this number only two per cent. had been convicted in Southern States. This condition of affairs can only be remedied by the juries of the country. I read a few days ago a statement from some writer who had visited several of the criminal courts of the country for the purpose of writing an article on what he had observed in regard to the practice in such courts. Among other things he stated that his observation had led him to conclude that when any one juror was taken three times in succession by the defense, he was a fit subject to sell a gold brick to. The usual defense in these cases is self-defense. Now, I see several murder cases on your docket. I know nothing of them but I can guess what the defense will be. It will be that 'the deceased put his hand to his hip pocket to shoot me, and I had to shoot him in self-defense' and it turns out that the deceased had no pistol. I can illustrate it by a story. . . . A fellow out West, who made a business of robbing graves and furnishing the bodies to a medical college for the young men to practice dissection on, had robbed a grave and was carrying the subject to the

68

college, and as he passed by a barroom, he saw quite a crowd in there drinking. He could not stand the temptation, and, standing the 'stiff' by the door, he went in and joined in the fun. After awhile a general row and a general shooting took place. During the fray, everybody got out except the bartender. After the smoke cleared away a 'cop,' strange to say, appeared upon the scene and saw the 'stiff' laying in the middle of the floor, where it had been thrown in the scuffle. He went up to the bartender and said to him, 'Why did you shoot this man?' The bartender said, 'Why he was about to draw his pistol to shoot me, and I had to shoot him in self-defense.' "

CRUDE WIT

There are on record many crude but witty addresses to juries. As the late Governor Morrow of Kentucky once said:

"The courts of justice in the mountains are not always show places of the English language, but native judges who may not know that LL.B. does not mean 'Lie like blazes,' often let fall gems of speech."

An unusual example is the charge which Circuit Judge Lou Lewis of the upper Kentucky River section gave to a grand jury. It was as follows: [5]

"Gentlemen of the jury: A most heinous crime has been called to the attention of this court. You all know the Piney Grove meetin' house. The godly elders and deacons thereof, in the goodness of their hearts went down to the banks of the middle forks of the Kentucky and with great care se-

69

lected a fine lot of water maples and brung 'em back and planted 'em in the meetin' house yard. Them trees growed and flourished and was doin' fine, but, gentlemen of the jury, observe the perversity of mankind. A few wild bucks on a Sunday rid their nags up to the meetin' house and, ignorin' the hitchin' post on the outside, rid their beasts into the yard and hitched them to the aforesaid maples and while the congregation inside wuz a-singin' sweet songs of Zion, them thar beasts chawed all the bark off uv them thar trees and totilly destroyed them. Gentlemen of the jury, I say to you that a man who would do the like uv that would ride a jackass into the Garden of Eden and hitch him to the Tree of Life. Indict 'em, gentlemen, indict 'em."

Another backwoods judge instructed a jury in the following vigorous terms: [6]

"I charge you if this act was done a-purpose, and done with such disregard of the rights of the plaintiff as to amount to wilfulness, then the jury has the right to apply the whip to the back of the defendant *company* in order to punish them."

THE SHORTEST CHARGES

Although a great many judges lay claim to having delivered the shortest charge, the honor seems to go to Mr. Justice Norris in the Calcutta High Court, who delivered what is understood to be the shortest summing-up on record. [7]

"Gentlemen of the jury, the prisoner has nothing to say, and I have nothing to say. What have you got to say?"

Another short instruction to a jury, according to the well-known legal magazine, *Ohio Law Reporter*, was

"that delivered by the late Commissioner Kerr at the Old Bailey in a case where a man was charged with being in the unlawful possession of a gold watch and chain.

"The appearance of the prisoner certainly did not correspond with the legitimate possession of such costly ornaments, but he asserted his innocence of the charge, and declared that he had found the watch and chain on the pavement.

"The judge looked at the man in the box.

" 'Gentlemen of the jury,' he said, 'I have walked over the pavements of London during the last forty years, and I've never found a gold watch and chain there yet. Consider your verdict.' "[8]

THE HIGH COST OF LAW

The late Sir William Maule delivered a sentence which is one of the most exquisite bits of satire in the law. A workman had been convicted of bigamy, and it appeared from the evidence that his wife had run off with a hawker five years before. Not having heard from her, he had married another woman. In imposing sentence, which was only for one day's imprisonment, Mr. Justice Maule said:[9]

"I will tell you what you ought to have done; and if you say you did not know, I must tell you that the law conclusively presumes that you *did*. You ought to have instructed your attorney to bring an action against the hawker for

71

criminal conversation with your wife. That would have cost you about one hundred pounds. When you had recovered substantial damages against the hawker you would have instructed your proctor to sue in the ecclesiastical courts for a divorce *a mensa atque thoro*. That would have cost you two or three hundred pounds more. When you had obtained a divorce *a mensa atque thoro*, you would have had to appear by counsel before the House of Lords for a divorce *a vinculo matrimonii*. The bill might have been opposed in all its stages in both houses of parliament, and altogether you would have had to spend eleven or twelve hundred pounds. You will probably tell me that you never had a thousand farthings of your own in the world; but, prisoner, that would make no difference. Sitting here as a British judge, it is my duty to tell you that this is not a country in which there is one law for the rich and another for the poor."

This master of satire, Sir William Maule, rendered another statement which should take its place in history among the unforgettable charges in the law. It read as follows:

"People talk about a man and his wife being one. It is all nonsense. I do not believe that under the most favorable circumstances they can be considered less than two. For instance, if a man murders his wife, did ever anybody hear of his having committed suicide? "

"THE REASONABLE DOUBT"

Most judges presiding over criminal cases have a great deal to say about the term "reasonable doubt." Edgar White's definition, as it appeared in the *Green Bag*, seems to be the best.

I'm the Reasonable Doubt,
Friend of the persecuted,
Enemy of the gallows
And the pen,
Twin relics of barbarism.
So raise all the hell you
   like—
Cut,
Slash,
Kill,
Waylay,
Grind your heels in their
   face;
Don't be afraid—
You'll find me there
At the trial,
Because
I'm the law.
When I get in among
Those twelve
Upright,
Honest,
Intelligent patriots,
Meaning the jury,
They'll see me,
And only me.
So what do you care?
Nobody this side
The Pearly Gates
Can tell
Just what I am.

Therefore they have to take
   me—
Sight unseen—
Blindly,
In the dark,
And give me the benefit
Of what they don't know
Which is lots.
But they'll do it;
It's the law,
Which has justice
Skinned a mile.
I stand for mercy for the
   living.
Let the dead lie
In peace.
He ought've dodged,
Or carried a gun himself,
Then maybe
I'd have given him a lift.
Get busy—
Shoot, stab, kill;
Jump on 'em.
Boil their grandmother in oil.
Tear your wife's eyes out,
Strangle your children,
Smash your best friend.
Turn the old world inside out;
Count on me.
Ever your friend,
Reasonable Doubt.

SOURCES

Chapter 5

1. *Mesa County Coop. Assn.* v. *McKinney*, 256 Pac. Rec. 13.

2. 10 Ohio Law Reporter 463.

3. Damnum Absque Injuria, by Frank M. Coppock.

4. *State* v. *Glenn*, 70 South Eastern Reporter, 453 at 454.

5. 18 Ohio Law Reporter 154.

6. *Harrison* v. *Western Union Telegraph Co.*, 75 S. C. 267; 55 S. E. 450 at 452.

7. Flashes of Wit, from Bench and Bar, by Wm. C. Sprague, p. 104.

8. 15 Ohio Law Reporter 518.

9. A String of Near Gems from the Law Reports, by Edwin Gholson.

CHAPTER 6

PECULIAR PENALTIES

"The hungry judges soon the sentence sign,
And wretches hang that jurymen may dine."

—Pope

THE USUAL penalties exacted by the law are so much taken for granted that they interest no one. Unusual penalties, however, are not often found recorded, and, when unearthed, they throw some weird highlights on history.

A BIGAMIST'S PUNISHMENT

During the reign of Philip II, there was recorded in the register of criminal sentences pronounced in Hondschoote, Flanders, a most unusual sentence.[1] A woman bigamist, by the name of Marie Ollivier, was ordered by court to wear two pairs of men's trousers around her neck for the remainder of her lifetime, so as to be constantly reminded of both husbands.

PENALTY WITHOUT CRIME

The laws of the earliest kings cite a most peculiar mandatory injunction which was issued in the year 930 during the reign of King Athelstan the Fifth. Every Friday, all of the monks in every monastery in England were required to sing fifty

76

psalms for the King.[2] Just why these servants of God were saddled with such a burden remains unexplained to this day.

PENALTY OF SILENCE

In the early part of the eighteenth century, the Reverend Sacheverill was sentenced by an English court "to keep silent for three years," according to the legal historian, John M. Zane, in *The Story of Law*, because he had preached two pro-Tory sermons which were extremely objectionable.[3]

HEAD PLOWING

An old law (Theat. Poen. II 271), cited by historian Dopler, condemned a man who dug up and without right removed a boundary stone to be buried in earth up to his neck; and to have his head plowed off with a new plow, thus symbolizing in his own person the grave offense which he had committed. The reason for this extreme penalty was that, in the early days, the right to own property was regarded as more important than the right to live. Hence this kind of barbaric punishment was tolerated many centuries.[4]

WOMEN WHO QUARREL

In 1348 a curious ordinance in effect at Dortmund, in Westphalia, Germany, required that:

". . . if two women quarrel so as to come to blows, and at the same time use abusive language, they shall be required to carry, the whole length of the town along the High Street, two stones weighing together 100 pounds, attached to chains. The first woman shall carry them from the east gate to the west gate, whilst the second goads her on with a needle fastened to the end of a stick. Both to wear the lightest of clothing."[5]

CONSISTENCY—HOBGOBLIN OF JUDGES

Strange penalties were accorded Babylonian judges who changed their legal opinions. Section 5 of the Code of Hammurabi provided:

"If a judge pronounces a judgment, renders a decision, delivers a verdict duly signed and sealed, and afterwards alters his judgment, they shall call that judge to account for the alteration of the judgment which he had pronounced and he shall pay twelvefold the penalty which was in said judgment; and in the assembly they shall expel him from his seat of judgment, and he shall not return, and with the judges in a case he shall not take his seat."[6]

WORK OR DIE

In his history of the ancient world, Herodotus quoted a strange law which Solon imposed on the Greeks after he had seen it enforced in Egypt. This law required that every man appear before his local Governor once a year to show his means of getting a livelihood; and if he failed to prove that he made an honest living he was put to death.

ORIGINAL POLE-SITTERS

For many centuries, in Germany, the punishment given one who had committed a minor crime was to cause him to sit all day on a pole in the middle of a canal with a tall scarlet steeple cap on his head. This kind of penalty seemed to be peculiar to the Germans, whose misdemeanants have often been referred to as the original pole-sitters![7]

All Greek law-proposers who appeared before legislative assemblies were required to wear a noose around their necks. If their proposed bill failed to pass, the proposer would instantly be hanged. This extreme penalty furnished a panacea for too many laws.

Zaleusus of the Epizephyrian Locrians was the author of this peculiar statute which has oftentimes been regarded as the most judicious law ever promulgated in Greece. People were less apt to propose foolish legislation, thereby saving everybody's time. It is interesting to observe that in Athens, if a law turned out badly, any citizen could bring a criminal action against the proposer.[8]

PENALTIES OF JURORS

During the sixteenth century, English juries were actually fined for acquitting anyone charged with crime. Probably the most outstanding case where jurors were fined was that of Sir Nicholas Throckmorton, in 1554. After a lengthy trial, an acquittal was brought in. For returning such a verdict, the jury was fined an amount equal to $39,000 and sentenced to Newgate prison.[9]

For many centuries, jurors sitting in English courts of law lost their citizenship and property if the verdicts which they returned were later set aside. Such extreme penalty naturally caused many to abhor the duty of serving on juries.[10]

During the reigns of Edward III and Henry IV and VI, any juror found eating and drinking without consent of the judge was imprisoned. This penalty was rigidly enforced and many jurors were incarcerated for having eaten while on duty. Blackstone fully discussed this phase of punishment in the third volume of his *Commentaries*.[11]

PENALIZED FOR EXTRAVAGANT APPAREL

During the reign of Edward III, common folk were forbidden to wear furs; all wives had to dress according to their husbands means (which was not such a bad law), and no Englishman could legally buy more than twelve hats abroad. In Ireland, there was a law which "forbiddeth any to weare theyre beardes on the upper lip and none under the chinn."[12]

THOU SHALT NOT BEAR FALSE WITNESS

According to Corpus Justinian, 667, when a witness was shown to be corrupt and malicious, Roman law required him to be thrown headlong from the high Tarpeian rock. Needless to say, very few ever survived.[13]

PUNISHMENT OF THE CHINESE IDOLS

One of the queerest punishments ever recorded in China involved fifteen wooden idols which were legally tried and convicted of murder in 1900. A prominent resident of Fouchow had been killed by an idol which had been pushed off the ledge of a temple. The "culprit" and its fourteen associates were ordered by a viceroy to be taken out of the temple and brought before the criminal court. This was done, and after trial was held the idols were sentenced to have their heads removed from their bodies and be thrown in a pond. The bloodless execution took place before a huge crowd which, according to reports, stood in awe.[14]

PUNISHMENT OF MARBLE STATUES

Marble statues have been the subject of a number of criminal prosecutions during the past centuries. The statue of Venus de Milo was tried for nudity in Mannheim, Germany, and sentenced to prison in 1853. The statue of the famous Greek Olympic champion, Theagenes, was tried for murder and sentenced to be drowned in the sea. This was after Theagenes had died and some of his enemies had pushed his statue from its pedestal—crushing a man to death.

PLOWSHARE PUNISHMENT

For centuries, the plowshare was used as an implement for the enforcement of legal decrees. In ancient times, as we have seen, the point of a plowshare settled the fate of those found guilty of removing boundary lines. In medieval times, if a man, while blindfolded, could walk over nine hot plowshares without getting burned, he won his case. This was one of the ordeals in a superstitious age and was known as trial by fire. From it developed the expression, "I'd go through fire and water for a friend," because in many instances a substitute was permitted to "take it" for the accused. Oftentimes a certain preparation was applied to the feet before the ordeal and burns were thereby prevented, thus insuring a verdict of acquittal. This form of trial had its origin among the Greeks and, during the time of Sophocles, was allowed only to persons of high rank.[15] Although this procedure was abolished in England in 1261, trial by ordeal is still legally practiced in Madagascar.[16]

THE METAL BRIDLE

Another implement ordered by courts during the eighteenth and nineteenth centuries to subdue common scolds was the metal bridle, known as the brank. This was an odd-looking metal strap which covered the mouths of female gossipers in England and Germany.

There was a brank on exhibition in the vestry of Walton-on-Thames Parish Church which the town of Chester presented in 1632 with the remarks:

"Chester presents Walton with a bridle
To curb women's tongue that talk too idle."

This penalty is now obsolete, although it remained legal in New Jersey as late as 1889. A Mrs. Mary Brady of Jersey

City was indicted by a grand jury as a common scold and her lawyers found that it was yet an indictable offense in that state, not having been abolished when the revised statutes were adopted. The ducking stool was still available as a penalty, too.[17]

HEAD BASKETS

In certain parts of Japan, men of "samurai" rank are still punished in the manner shown by the illustration. The reason for the basket over the head is to conceal the identity of the one convicted of a political crime. The flute is to attract attention of those passing by.[18]

TRAVELING ON THE SABBATH

An extract from Felt's *Annals of Salem* recites the penalty given two Salem men in 1638 who were found guilty of traveling on the Sabbath. They were ordered to "sit in the stocks all of Lecture day" by way of punishment.[19]

PUNISHMENT OF HUGUENOTS

When the Huguenots were driven out of France during the seventeenth century, many unusual punishments were ordered. In 1685, a Protestant chapel which stood in La Rochelle was ordered "to be demolished"; and its church bell "to be whipped, buried and disinterred," as punishment for having assisted heretics.[20] Obviously the bell's punishment was considerably harder on those who executed it than it was on the bell.

BOOK BURNING

The first instance in America where a "book was sentenced to be burned to death" took place in Salem, in 1695. Thomas Maule printed and published a two-hundred-and-sixty-page book entitled *Truth Held Forth and Maintained*. It dealt with the circumstances supposedly surrounding the death of Major General Atherton. Upon examination, Maule admitted the published account to be false, and hence the unusual sentence.[21]

GERMAN PETTY OFFENDERS

For many years in Germany, petty offenders were punished in a novel way. A dog was securely tied to the misdemeanant's shoulders and, with arms chained, the culprit was forced to run through neighboring towns and villages until full repentance became evident.[22] Just why the dog was made a necessary part of the sentence is unexplainable except that its bark may have helped attract the attention of curious onlookers.

The *Salem Gazette* reveals an amusing sentence which a Massachusetts court ordered in 1630. Josias Plastoree was found guilty of stealing four baskets of corn from the Indians, so he was obliged to return eight baskets, be fined five pounds and thereafter called the name of Josias, "not Mister as formerly he used to be."[23]

MILK DRINKING

The gruesome punishment illustrated was meted out to those in France during the fifteenth century who were found guilty of selling adulterated milk in violation of the original French Fraud Statute of Louis XI. The offenders were literally forced to drink their own diluted product until a doctor certified that they could not swallow any more without endangering life.[24]

ROGER BACON'S PUNISHMENT

Six hundred and fifty years ago, the great English philosopher, Roger Bacon, was sentenced by a court to remain in solitary confinement in a prison in Paris "because he had allegedly disturbed the peace of the world" by predicting the use of airplanes and steamboats.[25]

WILLIAM PENN'S PUNISHMENT

William Penn was sent to prison by a British judge sitting in Old Bailey Hall, on September 1, 1670, because he refused to pay a fine imposed upon him for wearing his hat while in court.[26]

VOLTAIRE'S PUNISHMENT

Voltaire was ordered flogged, in 1751, by Frederick III, King of Prussia, and required to give a legal receipt which read as follows: [27]

"Received from the right hand of Conrad Bochoffner thirty lashes on my bare back, being *in full* for an epigram on Frederick III, King of Prussia, *Vive le Roi.*

                    (Signed) Arouet de Voltaire."

THE GUILLOTINER GUILLOTINED

James Douglas, Lord Regent of Scotland, was responsible for bringing the guillotine into Scotland from England, and he was among the first to lose his head on it. King James VI charged Douglas (fourth Earl of Morton) with complicity in murdering his father, husband of Queen Mary Stuart. After trial and conviction, in 1581, Douglas was decapitated on the same guillotine which he had introduced into Scotland years before. It was known as the "Scottish Maiden" and came from Halifax.[28]

PRESSING FOR AN ANSWER

The kind of torture illustrated was known as "pressing one for an answer," and for almost four centuries suspected criminals were actually forced in this way to plead their innocence or guilt. History records the case of Thomas Spigot who endured over four hundred pounds of weight before answering a plea of not guilty to a charge of murder. The system remained in operation in England until 1772.[29]

A RIFLE SENTENCED

A rifle was sentenced to death in Scotland in 1782. Squire Drun and his rifle were jointly indicted for murder. The Sheriff's court in Edinburgh conducted the hearing and acquitted Drun. The court convicted the rifle, however, as it was shown that the weapon was instrumental in causing the death of the decedent. The life of the rifle was subsequently ordered forfeited to the crown.[30]

THE PUNISHMENT THAT MADE A LAWYER

Mr. Sergeant Davey, who now lies buried in Surrey, England, died in 1780. He is remembered by an unusual incident.

A process server had attempted to serve Mr. Davey (then a chemist at Exeter) but was required to swallow the writ of parchment he was about to serve. Davey had offered the process server some drinks, during which time he heated a poker and told the sheriff's officer that if he did not eat up the writ, he'd be forced to swallow the poker. The bailiff swallowed the writ, but the Court of Common Pleas in Westminster Hall, not then accustomed to Mr. Davey's jokes, sent for him, read him a serious lecture on contempt of their process, and locked him up in Fleet prison.

It is interesting to note that, because of this incident, Mr. Davey acquired a taste for the law (which the writ had not given to the process server) and, when discharged from jail, studied law, was called to the bar, made a sergeant and remained in practice of law for many years.[31]

MASSACHUSETTS PUNISHMENTS

Some curious punishments took place in the early seventeenth century in Massachusetts. The following province laws were in force in 1686:

"Public swearing, hot iron through tongue;

For kissing a woman in the street, offender tied to a gun in or at the Town Hall and whipped at the direction of the Magistrate;

Common scolds to be gagged and tied to their own door steps for certain hours so as to permit all comers and goers to gaze at them."[32]

CARDINAL WOLSEY'S PUNISHMENT

It may surprise many readers to know that Cardinal Wolsey was convicted of rioting when he was twenty-nine years of age, and by way of punishment was forced to sit in the stocks.

Wolsey, sometimes known as the "boy bachelor," because he had secured his bachelor's degree when only fifteen years of age, was tried by a Justice of the Peace by the name of Sir Amyas Pawlet, in Somersetshire, Lymington Parish, near Ilchester, England, in the year 1500, for drunkenness while attending a fair. The Court convicted him "on the view" and ordered him to be set in the stocks which, according to the writer, Cavandish, were still standing in his time, near the Magdalen Church. The sentence was carried into immediate effect. Legal history records that Wolsey, upon later attaining the office of Chancellor of England, took out his revenge upon the Justice of the Peace who perpetrated such a conviction upon him. Wolsey enjoined Pawlet from departing without leave or license and virtually detained him a prisoner in the Gate House of the Middle Temple, next to Fleet Street, for five years.[33]

AN AUTHOR FORCED TO EAT HIS OWN WORDS

The bizarre performance pictured took place in 1819, in Russia. The unfortunate author was tried amid a tremendous crowd, resulting in a conviction, the sentence being to "eat his own words" page by page. A scaffold was then erected in the main street, and the imperial provost, in the presence of the judges, Czar's physician, and assembly, separated the book from its binding, rolled up each leaf, and presented it to the author for consumption. Three days were required to complete the sentence.[34]

SADISM?

Many forms of punishment in the past have been designed to satisfy sadistic tastes. Unfortunately, penalties which seem to me similar have not been entirely dispensed with by our present-day courts. On July 6, 1932, pursuant to a sentence imposed by Common Pleas Judge Robert N. Putnam, of Millersburg, Holmes County, Ohio, two brothers who pleaded guilty to stealing an ice-box from an empty house, and selling it for three dollars, were given twenty lashes each, before a crowd of three hundred townspeople. Having been ordered by the court to take either twenty days in the workhouse on a diet of bread and water, or receive twenty lashes, Jesse and William Wynn elected the lashing. The brothers, securely handcuffed, were tied to the cell bars of the county jail on the edge of the town's public park, and Sheriff John (Peg) Stevens wielded the whip, administering the flogging in strict compliance with the court's instruction.[35]

The reports indicate that the three hundred citizens who

gathered to watch the punishment booed at first, and then later stood overawed in silence. Although neither of the convicted men appeared to suffer severely, the powerful sheriff twice broke the light buggy-whip on the younger brother and had to finish the punishment with a "blacksnake" lash. The prisoners were subsequently led to the county line, and, on instructions from the court, ordered never to return. Such a spectacle was a scene nobody would expect to witness today.

During prohibition days, various police judges sitting in the large-sized cities penalized prisoners found guilty of being habitual drunkards by ordering them to drink publicly a pint of castor oil. Since the repeal of prohibition, "castor oil" sentences have fortunately become penalties of the past.

Such extreme penalties were legally justified on the ground that the punishments were the alternative of a jail sentence and were at the election of the "culprit."

TRESPASSERS "PERSECUTED"

Before concluding this chapter some reference should be made to the most humorous trespass sign ever erected. It was posted near Tia Juana, Mexico, a few years ago, and illustrates to what lengths a disgruntled property-owner will go.

NOTIS
trespassers will B persecuted to the full extent of 2 mungrel dogs which never was sochible to strangers 4 I dubble brl shot gun which aint loded with sofa pillors. Dam if I aint gitten tired of this hell raisin on my place.
B. GRISCOM.

SOURCES
Chapter 6

1. Registre des Sentences Criminelles Executées in Hondschoote sous le Regne de Phillippe II.

2. The Laws of the Earliest Kings, by F. L. Attenborough, p. 155.

3. The Story of Law, by John M. Zane, Ives Washburn, Inc., pp. 381, 382.

4. Criminal Prosecutions, by E. P. Evans, p. 182.

5. Strange Pains and Penalties, pp. 97, 98.

6. The Laws of Moses and the Code of Hammurabi, by S. A. Cook.

7. Curiosities of Olden Times, by S. Baring-Gould, pp. 98, 99.

8. The Story of Law, by John M. Zane, Ives Washburn, Inc., p. 405.

9. Curiosities of Law and Lawyers, by Thomas Frost, pp. 123, 124.

10. Reading on History and System of Common Law (3 Ed.), by Pound & Plucknett, chap. VII, pp. 434, 435; also The Older Modes of Trial, by James B. Thayer, 5 H. L. R. (2) p. 379.

11. Blackstone's Commentaries, Vol. iii, pp. 387, 388.

12. Sumptuary Laws, by Francis Watt, p. 134.

13. Slander and Libel (2), by Martin L. Newell, p. 4.

14. Criminal Prosecution and Capital Punishment, by E. P. Evans, p. 174.

15. Trials in Superstitious Ages, by Ernest H. Rann.

16. Americana, Vol. XX, pp. 752, 753.

17. Some Obsolete Peculiarities of English Law, by Wm. Beamont, pp. 36-41.

18. Japanese Criminal Records.

19. Strange and Curious Punishments, by Henry M. Brooks, p. 8.

20. Benoit's Histoire de l'Edit de Nantes, p. 754.

21. Strange and Curious Punishments, by Henry M. Brooks, pp. 15, 16.

22. Strange Pains and Penalties.

23. Strange and Curious Punishments, by Henry M. Brooks, pp. 34, 35.

24. Statute of Louis XI (1481).

25. The Library of Historic Characters and Famous Events, by A. R. Spoffard, Vol. X, pp. 158-161.

26. Romantic Trials of Three Centuries, by Hugh Childers, p. 55.

27. Old Time Punishments, by Wm. Andrews, p. 103.

28. Dictionary of National Biography, Vol. 5, p. 1226.

29. Old Time Punishments, by Wm. Andrews, pp. 206, 208.

30. History of Scotland's Sheriff's Courts.

31. Law and Lawyers—Curious Facts and Characteristic Sketches, by D. L. Purves, pp. 9, 10.

32. Strange and Curious Punishments, by Henry M. Brooks, pp. 19, 20.

33. Lives of the Lord Chancellors, Vol. 1, pp. 366-367.

34. Strange and Curious Punishments, by Henry M. Brooks, pp. 66, 68.

35. State of Ohio v. Jesse Wynn, et al. (1932), Holmes County, Ohio.

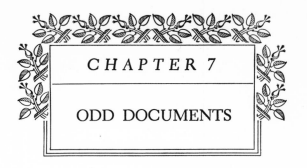

CHAPTER 7

ODD DOCUMENTS

"The sparks of all the sciences in the world are taken up in the ashes of the law."

—Sir Henry Finch

AN ARIZONA ARREST

SOME of the driest humor to be found anywhere appears in law records. The following return made by a deputy in a sheriff's office is an example:[1]

Received the within process at Arizona City, Jan. 1873 and served same by arresting defendant at Ehrenberg A. T., Jan. 31, 1873, but as defendant had no money and I was broke myself and the county don't pay cash in advance, and no steamboat around and no calaboose here and defendant wouldn't walk down to Yuma all alone by himself and I wouldn't walk down with him as he wouldn't stay arrested unless I boarded him which I had no money for to do, and as he gave up the coat (value 45 cents currency—estimated) and said he never stole it but Bryson was a damned liar anyhow, and not knowing what to do with him, I did nothing more to him to date beyond giving him excellent moral advice which he assured me was entirely unnecessary in his case, his life having been blameless and his reputation spotless as he could prove by the best men in Nevada and Idaho

96

but have allowed him to run at large until a more favorable season when a steamboat happens to be here, and will take script for his passage to Yuma and present the bill to Supervisors themselves, which is nearly all I have done toward serving within process, though I would make return of the balance were this process bigger on the back.

Fees—Balance of what coat sells for after paying Justice fees.

(signed) George Tyng,
Sheriff of Yuma County,
ARIZONA

DEEDED TO GOD

One of the queerest deeds on record was executed June 14, 1864, by a religious couple living near Laporte, Pennsylvania. The document conveyed to Almighty God about six hundred acres of farm land located in Sullivan County, Pennsylvania.

The present Recorder of Sullivan County certifies that the deed is on record in his office at Laporte, Pennsylvania, having been recorded August 3, 1864.

A true copy of the instrument reads as follows:[2]

THIS INDENTURE made the fourteenth day of June, in the year of our Lord one thousand eight hundred and sixty-four, PETER E. ARMSTRONG and Wife to ALMIGHTY GOD, know all men by these presents, that I, Peter E. Armstrong and Hanna, my wife, of the County of Sullivan and State of Pennsylvania, having redeemed from the inhabitants of Earth, by lawful purchase, a certain tract of land within the boundaries herein described, and being fully impressed and taught by the Inspired Word of God and His Holy Spirit that His children should not claim to own prop-

97

erty of any kind as individuals, but that they should render and consecrate unto God all things that they possess for the common good of His people who are waiting for His Son from Heaven and who are willing to live together in holy fellowship, relying upon His word and bounty; and to the end that His saints may be fully separated from the world and gather and enjoy that light and liberty which they did in the once faithful days of their theocracy, we do make and establish this deed of conveyance this fourteenth day of June in the year of our Lord one thousand eight hundred and sixty-four.

WHEREAS, in consideration of the kind, protecting care of Almighty God in the past and present, which we do hereby acknowledge, and for the exceeding great and precious promise of unending life to those who in holy faith and patience wait for the coming of His anointed Son to judge the world, which promises we have received from him who is creator and original grantor of earth's territory to the children of men, we do, by these presents, deed, grant and convey to ALMIGHTY GOD, who inhabiteth Eternity, and to His Heirs in Jesus Messiah, to the intent that it shall be subject to bargain and sale by man's cupidity no more forever, all our right and title (by human law), interest and claim of any nature soever in or to, of that certain tract of land and improvements thereof lying and being in the County of Sullivan and State of Pennsylvania, being our part of a parcel of land within the following bounds:

BEGINNING at a point in the wilderness three hundred and twenty rods due South of the Southwest corner of the town plot of Celestia (as recorded in Deed Book No. 2, page 266, in the office for the recording of deeds in and for the County of Sullivan), and running due West three hundred and twenty perches to a corner; thence due North six hundred and forty rods to a corner; thence due East six hundred and forty rods to a corner; thence due South six hundred and forty rods to a corner; thence due West three hundred and twenty rods to the place of beginning. Containing four square miles of land, of which we have redeemed about six hundred acres, and we do hereby set apart by boundary with intent to redeem the balance of said tract at or before the redemption of the world, as the purchased possession of Jesus Messiah, together with all and singular the rights, liberties, privileges and appurtenances whatsoever thereunto belonging to us. We do grant, deed, and convey to the said CREATOR and GOD OF HEAVEN AND EARTH and to His Heirs in Jesus Messiah, for their proper use and behoof forever.

IN WITNESS WHEREOF, we have hereunto set our hands and seals this day and year above written.

Sealed in the presence of John S. Green, J.P.

(signed) PETER E. ARMSTRONG
HANNA ARMSTRONG

The property now forms a part of the Pennsylvania game preserve.

DEEDED TO JEHOVAH GOD

Another document deeding land to God is now on record in the recorder's office at Washington, Indiana. On November 30, 1935, three hundred and twenty acres of land were deeded to "Jehovah God." The terms of this peculiar transfer are set out in full: [3]

No. 377—Declaration of purpose and intention with reference to property, monies and income.

Appreciating that man exists upon the earth, which physical signs such as the beautiful flowers, stately trees, mists and rains for watering the herbs of the earth and producing the mighty rivers all go to show a love and provision was made for man's benefit and blessing (Psa. 19:1, 4). All this shows a great design far superior to that which man can create (Psa. 19:7-9). Reasoning that man likes to receive returns from his efforts and works; appreciation should look for some means for returning an indication of such love and benevolence of a living, wise designer and law-giver. Also same reasoning should show us that such a being or power that could design and write such laws as that which man commonly calls nature, would also have knowledge how to convey to His thankful creatures His will and how the design of His creation should be run (Gen. 2:15-17). Such a law is written in the Book of Books called the Bible; which study now shows that the time has now come when it has begun to reveal to the thankful of heart its secrets. (Pro. 3:32-35.) Searchers of the Bible will find that the Creator has revealed Himself to the obedient by the name of Jehovah about 7000 times in the Bible; but is generally translated "Lord" with capital letters. And that the name of Jehovah means that in his due time he does special purposes toward his people. Diligent search also shows that Jehovah claims the earth as His (Ecc. 9:29; Psa. 24:1), and expects order and obedience as to how it shall be run. (Deu. 11:26-28; Jer. 7:23; Jer. 11:4, 7.) The Bible also shows why there is so much evil, suffering and death in the earth. It reveals that originally man was made perfect and designed to live forever upon the earth in a perfect state of contentment and happiness (Gen. 3:22-24). It further reveals that Jehovah set one of His highly intelligent, spiritual creatures over man to be man's instructor, guide and helper (Ezek. 28:14-19); that this intelligent angel, originally called Lucifer, coveted the worship of man above Jehovah (Mat. 4:8-10); (Isa. 14:12-14); persuaded man to disobey Jehovah's just laws (Gen. 3:1-7) and challenged Jehovah to put men upon earth that would maintain their faithfulness or integrity (Job. 2:3, 7). For such rebellion Jehovah promised a curse upon man and sentenced him to death, and promised in his due time he would take the rulership away from Lucifer, now Jehovah's opponent (Satan), and destroy him (Gen. 3:14-19; Heb. 2:14-18) and resurrect obedient man to everlasting life (Mat. 22:32; Luke 10:28). And now realizing that the physical facts as revealed in the scriptures, show that Satan's rulership over the world must have legally ended in 1914 when the great trouble began to come upon the Devil's world or arraignment as foretold by Christ Jesus in his great prophecy (Mat. 24th chapter); (also in Dan. 12:1; Rev. 11:17, 18). Since we are to render unto Caesar the things that are Caesar's and unto Jehovah God the things that are God's (Mat. 22:21; Rom. 13:7-14); and seeing that the earth is Jehovah's (Isa. 34:1-8); and that it shall not be sold forever (Lev. 25:23); that man at his best is just a steward (Luke 12:42; 16:1-8); and the undersigned having been deeded a lifetime interest, according to the laws of mankind, in: the east half of Section 8, in the Township 4 North, of Range 7 west in Steel Township, Daviess County, Indiana, for the consideration of Jehovah's love, guidance and preservation, and his sustaining grace to serve him, I do hereby execute and deed to Jehovah God my lifetime interest, according to the former deed, and dedicate the returns and rentals and proceeds of said land to be used for the benevolent purpose of advertising as a witness to the world of mankind the knowledge that Jehovah is Lord of the Earth (Isa. 43:10-21); that He has set His obedient and faithful son Christ Jesus as earth's rightful ruler, and that all mankind who love Jehovah

101

and righteousness should flee to that Kingdom by giving their full allegiance and obedience to that Kingdom; and that Satan's world or arraignment has legally come to an end (Psa. 2:1-12). I further designate that as a steward of said land I shall render to Zion (Psa. 2:6; Rev. 14:1), Jehovah Universal Organization and to the Watch Tower Bible and Tract Society as a visible part of that organization the proceeds after my meager necessities are met, and further designate that said lands shall be held in trust by me as steward until my death, or until the return of said Princess (Ancient Prophets), as designated in Psa. 45:16; Heb. 11:2-40.

WITNESS my hand and affirmation (Mat. 5:34-37) this 30th. day of November, 1935.

(signed) SETH A. KEITH

State of Indiana \
County of Lawrence } ss.

Before me, the undersigned, a Notary Public, in and for said county and State, this 30th. day of Nov. A.D. 1935, personally appeared the within named Seth A. Keith, Grantor in the above conveyance, and acknowledged the same to be his voluntary act and deed, for the uses and purposes herein mentioned. In witness whereof, I have hereunto subscribed my name and affixed my official seal.

(signed) Helen F. Evans \
Notary Public

SIR FRANCIS DRAKE'S BRASS PLATE

Another odd document is the plate of brass left in 1579 by Sir Francis Drake, upon taking possession of what is now California. In the fall of 1577, Drake sailed from England bound for the Orient. A year later he passed through the

Strait of Magellan and eventually put into San Francisco Bay which, according to an account of his chaplain, who wrote *The World Encompassed*, he found to be a satisfactory harbor.

This brass plate was discovered in 1936, and a year later authenticated by the California Historical Society. It reads:

BEE IT KNOWNE VNTO ALL MEN BY THESE
PRESENTS
IVNE 17, 1579.
BY THE GRACE OF GOD AND IN THE NAME OF HERR MAIESTY QUEEN ELIZABETH OF ENGLAND AND HERR SVCESSORS FOREVER I TAKE POSSESSION OF THIS KINGDOME WHOSE KING AND PEOPLE FREELY RESIGNE THEIR RIGHT AND

TITLE IN THE WHOLE LAND VNTO HERR MAIES-
TIES KEEPING. NOW NAMED BY ME AN TO BEE
KNOWNE VNTO ALL MEN AS NOVA ALBION.

C. FRANCIS DRAKE

It now belongs to the University of California, where it
may be found on exhibition.[4]

THE WORLD'S LONGEST LEASE

Alphonso Taft, father of the late president, drafted the
longest term lease in the world. It ran for 10,000 years, re-
newable forever.

This remarkable lease, drawn January 1, 1849, was given
by the president, trustees and faculty of the College of Cincinnati to the Young Men's Mercantile Library Association.
It is recorded in the Hamilton County Recorder's Office in
Cincinnati, Ohio.[5]

A STEEL CHECK

A steel check, weighing over twelve pounds and measur-
ing a foot high and two feet long, passed as legal tender in
1932.

104

The most startling fact about this peculiar check is that the bank which cashed it canceled it with a rifle. If you look closely, you will observe that the letters in the word PAID were formed by bullet holes. The check was given by a certain electrical company in Cleveland to the winner of one of its arc-welding contests. Despite the weight and size, a local bank put the fifteen-hundred-dollar steel check through clearance after the payee endorsed his name on the reverse side by means of a welding rod.[6]

A WOODEN CHECK

Another unusual check was written on a wooden shingle, on February 18, 1935, in Goodwater, Alabama, by B. Gay of the Goodwater Hardware Company, to the order of Jeff McCord, in the sum of $36.75, for furnishing certain lumber dressing. The shingle was endorsed to the Alabama Power Company which deposited it with the Peoples Trust Savings Bank. Immediately thereafter, the bank honored the shingle check as legal tender.[7]

105

A CLOTH CHECK

On April 18, 1913, the Star Palace Laundry, of Rochester, New York, drew a $2,000 check on the bosom of a dress shirt to the order of the Y. M. C. A. Fund. This strange "negotiable paper" was put through clearance by the Alliance Bank and is believed to be the only check of its kind in existence.[8]

A TWO-VOLUME COMPLAINT

Still another odd document was a petition drafted in 1905 for the Brooklyn Teachers Association and the Class Teachers Organization of Brooklyn. The complaint, said to be the longest one ever found, was against the Board of Education of New York City. The pleading was bound in two volumes, each of the size of the Standard Dictionary. Thirty-four hundred and fourteen separate causes of action were set out, each representing an assignment to the plaintiffs of a claim of a teacher for salary under certain schedules. It took seven months to draft, and covered three thousand four hundred and fourteen pages.[9]

A POETIC BRIEF

In *14 Ohio Law Reporter 73*, there appears a brief in poetry. It was filed in the Fayette County Common Pleas Court in the case of Ralph Strobel, plaintiff in error, versus W. E. Maynard, defendant in error. It reads:

The sages of old with reason assumed
The shorter the horse the sooner he's groomed;
And so with this case and the questions involved,
They're exceedingly brief and speedily solved.

The Plaintiff below was a broker, it seems,
And perhaps being broke, saw a fee in his dreams,
He had from one Ellis a small farm to sell
And likewise, from Strobel, a town lot as well.

One day on the street by accident strange
He met Mr. Strobel and proposed an exchange.
He also, quite prudently, spoke of the fee
And told Brother Strobel how much it would be.

He stated both principals ought to agree
On the portion each party would pay of said fee.
"Very well," then said Strobel, "I'll trade for his farm,
And as for your fee, have not an alarm."

"Go straight and see Ellis and get him to say
How much of said fee he'll be willing to pay."
The broker then started to see Mr. Ellis,
And now his reply Brother Ellis will tell us:

"I'll pay just $2, and no more," said he;
"Of the said $16 you charge as your fee.
If Strobel won't trade upon that I'd as well
Keep my money and let the old trade go for a spell."

Then the broker returned and reported to Strobel
Who sanctioned the terms in these words grand and noble
"$2 from 16 leaves 14 for me
And this I will pay you, to make up your fee;

"Day-after-tomorrow I'll pay you a V
And the rest in installments—to this I agree;
Go close up the deal as soon as can be,
The sooner the better for you and for me."

So the deal was soon closed and the deeds passed, you bet
But that "day after tomorrow" has never come yet
And that was the day Strobel promised to pay
The first V installment in such a sure way.

The evidence shows that when Strobel sent
The broker to see Mr. Ellis, he went
And did everything he required that he should
And tried to get Ellis to pay all he could.

And now, I submit, your Honor, to you,
In absence of proof to a contrary view,
The law will presume good faith in this case
And order the broker to win in the race.

(signed) W. E. MAYNARD
Washington Court House, Ohio.

CRUIKSHANK'S BANK NOTE

In the early nineteenth century, hanging was the penalty meted out to those who passed forged pound notes in England. In 1818, the famed caricaturist, George Cruikshank, witnessed some violators strung up near Old Bailey Prison in London. As a protest he designed the note illustrated. It created a great sensation. At once bank directors held frantic meetings. Further issuance of pound notes was prohibited and consequently there were no more hangings for passing forged one-pound notes.[10]

AN EXPENSIVE BONFIRE

At the turn of this century, there occurred one of the most expensive bonfires in history. "One of the English railway

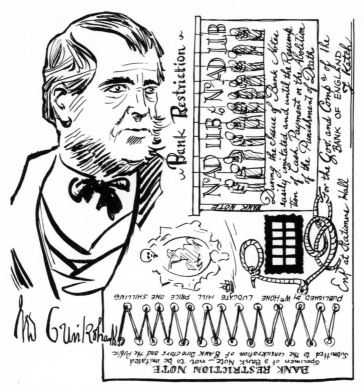

companies," says the *Ohio Law Reporter*, vol. 2, page 444, "made a bonfire of all documents in legal proceedings to which the company had been made a party during the period from 1837 to 1880. The papers weighed over five tons. It was estimated that their preparation cost the company not less than $35,000,000."

THE WORLD'S LONGEST DEED

The longest manuscript deed in the world is 135 feet in length. It was discovered in 1926 and at present hangs suspended from a wire in the Royal Library at Cairo. This unique conveyance, known as a Mohammedan trust-deed, dates from the fifteen hundreds and establishes a trust in favor of the grantor's heirs and freedmen.[11]

PROPERTY TRACED TO ADAM AND EVE

A chapter on odd documents would not be complete without a reference to the deed which traces back to Adam and Eve the chain of title to certain property. It reads as follows:[12]

THIS INDENTURE, made the 9th. day of October in the year of our Lord 1793, between Clara Helena Ellinkhuysen, of the town of Louisberg in the township of Buffaloe, in the county of Northumberland, and Commonwealth of Pennsylvania, widow, of the one part, and Flavel Roan, of the town of Sunbury, in the county of Commonwealth aforesaid, Esquire, of the other part.

WHEREAS, the Creator of the earth, by parole and livery of seizin, did enfeoff the parents of mankind, to-wit, Adam and Eve, of all that certain tract of land, called and known in the planetary system by the name of the Earth, together with all and singular the advantages, woods, waters, watercourses, easements, liberties, privileges, and all others the appurtenances whatsoever, thereunto belonging, or in any wise apertaining, to have and to hold to them the said Adam and Eve, and the heirs of their bodies lawfully to be begotten, in fee-tail general forever, as by the said feoffment recorded by Moses in the first chapter of the first book of his records, commonly called Genesis, more fully at large appears on reference being thereunto had;

AND WHEREAS, the said Adam and Eve died seized of

the premises aforesaid in fee tail general, leaving issue, heirs of the body, to-wit, sons and daughters, who entered into the same premises and became thereof seized as tenants in common by virtue of the donations aforesaid, and multiplies their seed upon the earth;

AND WHEREAS, in process of time, the heirs of the said Adam and Eve having become very numerous, and finding it to be inconvenient to remain in common aforesaid, bethought themselves to make partition of the lands and tenements aforesaid to and amongst themselves, and they did accordingly make such partition;

AND WHEREAS, by virtue of the said partition made by the heirs of the said Adam and Eve, all that certain tract of land called and known on the general plan of the said Earth by the name of America, parcel of the said large tract, was allotted and set over unto certain of the heirs aforesaid, to them and to their heirs general in fee simple who entered into the same and became thereof sized as aforesaid in their demesne as of fee, and peopled the same allotted lands in severalty and made partition thereof to and amongst their descendants;

AND WHEREAS, afterwards (now deemed in time immemorial) a certain united people called "The Six Nations of North America" heirs and descendants of the said grantees of America, became seized, and for a long time whereof the memory of time runneth not to the contrary, have been seized in their demesne as of fee, of and in a certain tract of county and land in the north division of America, called and known at present on the general plan of the said north division by the name of Pennsylvania;

AND WHEREAS, the said united nations, being so thereof seized, afterwards, to-wit, in the year of our Lord 1668, by their certain deed of feoffment with livery of seizen,

111

MARRIAGE LICENSE.

The State of Illinois,
Peoria County, ss.
To the World
Greeting

Know Ye that John Smith and Poly Myers is hereby entitled to go together and do as old folks does anywhere inside Coppers precinct — and when my commission comes, I am to marry 'em good and date 'em back to kiver accidents

OMR 1840
Justice of the Peace

112

did grant, bargain, sell, release, enfeoff, alienate and confirm unto Thomas Penn and Richard Penn, otherwise called the Proprietaries of Pennsylvania (among other things), the country called Buffaloe Valley, situate on the south side of the west branch of the Susquehanna, parcel of said country called Pennsylvania, to hold to them the said proprietaries, their heirs and assigns forever, in their demesne as of fee, as by the same feoffment more fully appears; which last mentioned tract of country was, afterwards, with other tracts of country, by the said proprietaries by the advice and consent of their council in general assembly met, erected into a county called Northumberland aforesaid, of which the said Buffaloe Valley was and is parcel by the name of Buffaloe township aforesaid;

AND WHEREAS, et cetera.

Recorded November 3, 1793

in Deed Book F on page 280.

> State of Pennsylvania
> Northumberland County } ss:
> Certified from the Recorder's office of Northumberland County under my hand and the seal of said office, at Sunbury, Pa. this 21st. day of
> SEAL   April, A.D. 1939.
> (Signed) JOHN I. CARR,
> Recorder

A RETROACTIVE MARRIAGE LICENSE

The marriage license on page 112 was discovered recently in the archives of the clerk's office of Fulton County, Illinois. It was executed in 1840 by a Justice of the Peace of Peoria County, Illinois, and is undoubtedly the most singular instrument of its kind in the world.[13]

On December 4, 1928, three residents of Chicago incorporated the Noah's Ark Exploration Association under the Not-for-Profit Act of Illinois, for the following purpose, among others, "to explore for and find anything pertaining to Noah's Ark, tangible and or intangible." The charter is on file in the office of the Secretary of State in Springfield, Illinois.[14]

MR. PHILPOTT CHANGES HIS NAME

In the year 1888, George Vere Hobart Philpott filed an application for change of name in the county court of Chautauqua, New York. His petition is as amusing as it was convincing.[15]

The petition of GEORGE VERE HOBART PHIL-POTT respectfully represents unto this honorable court at Hawkesbury, Cape Breton, Nova Scotia, on the 17th. day of January, 1865, your petitioner was born and straightway, he

had thrust upon him the cumbersome and mirth-provoking
name by him, amidst the jeers and taunts of an unfeeling
kind, for near the fourth of a century, borne in seeming forti-
tude and he hopes with rectitude, and by which now being of
full age and a permanent resident of this State and of the
said county of Chautauqua, he now petitions for such relief
in the premises as is agreeable to equity and good conscience,
that he may be lawfully stripped of his surname, and as
George Vere Hobart, from then, thenceforth and forever be
known, because and for that the first syllable of the surname
of your petitioner, when pronounced as phonetically spelled
and then associated with the last syllable thereof, suggests to
that vast and humorously inclined portion of the common
public, many and annoying calembours upon utensils more
or less intimately connected with the household and the
kitchen, of many metals and divers wares, which by many
quibbles, much play on words, and certain presumed apt expressions, with exasperating laughter and self-satisfied smiles,
with never ending and ever varying changes constantly rung
upon degrees of emptiness and fullness, and pots and kettles
of all manner of use and kind, from the humble yet seductive
jack-pot unto those of tinkling brass, "up and down and all
around they hammer away like a nailer," with much synthetic
reasoning and synonyms galore, until both puns and punsters
unto your petitioner are moss-grown and ivy covered in their
antiquity. And again, innocently, persons who never dreamed
a pun, nor would they know one if they saw it, having never
heard the name, right common too in England, are at a loss
how to proceed therewith, contract the same by speech and
pen into all manner of shapes and forms and combinations
of sounds, vowels, consonants and combinations of the alpha-
bet, and the name the forefathers of your petitioner bore in
honor, resignation, England and Nova Scotia where the good

people are more staid and less humorously inclined, straightway is a byword in the land and in the mouth of the unrefined, and is, in many renderings lost in identity, and your petitioner, by ignorant metamorphosis, is MR. PHILLIP POTT, FILLPOT or worse than all, FULL POT, in which pseudonyme those same humorously inclined and many friends with a keen sense of the ridiculous find much themselves and admiring auditors to please, and many suggestions of the simposium, and the more vulgar ones, by tentative and that same synthetic reasoning and apt association of ideas and things, are led to commonplace expressions relative the "growler" whatever that same may be, and by quick transition, unto the chasing thereof.

WHEREFORE, with no disposition to lessen the sum of human happiness, having passed through the stages of "infancy and schoolboy days" now proudly treading the busy stage of manhood; having stood the "taunts and jeers of outrageous fortune" through all those years of puns and punishment for no wrong by him committed; desiring a name that in this cosmopolitan country will add dignity to rather than detract from a promise to pay, through the conscience of this honorable court, he seeks an equalization of amusement and protection in the years to come as he glides down or struggles up the pathway of life, as the fates decree, toward a setting sun, feeling that this honorable court will presume, for the reasons aforesaid and believe with him that the "foul deeds" which may by him have been committed, or by those who came before him, lived like him afflicted, and died without an epitaph, for what will rhyme with pot, even unto the third and fourth generation, are outlawed or have in the crucible of puns been "burnt and purged away," your petitioner entreats the granting of his request and your petitioner will ever pray.

The attorneys for the petitioner were Smith & Brown, of 410 Fayette Street, Jamestown, N. Y. Needless to say, the court granted the application and ordered Mr. Philpott to abandon his last name and forever assume the appellation of George Vere Hobart, thereby avoiding all future "taunts and jeers."

A RAZOR-BACK ON A RAILROAD TRACK

In 1915, a farmer living in Sioux County, Iowa, filed a complaint in the District Court against a certain railroad company for having run over his pig. The petition read: [16]

```
      My razor-back strolled down your track
        One cold December day.
      Your 69 came down the line
        And snuffed his life away.
      You can't blame me, the swine you see,
        Stole thru your broken fence—
      So send me check for twenty-five
        The debt to recompense.
```

Not to be outdone, the attorneys representing the railroad company drafted and filed the following answer:

The jury returned a verdict in favor of the plaintiff, Jacob DeVries, awarding him $18.56 for the "life" which was "snuffed away."

117

```
Our 69 went down the line
  And killed your swine, we know,
But razor-backs on R.R. tracks
  Quite often come to woe.
The check for 25 we do decline
  For which your heart doth pine;
Just plant the dead, place o'er his head,
  "HERE LIES A FOOLISH SWINE."
```

THE SMALLEST REAL ESTATE TRANSACTION IN HISTORY

Back in the early nineties, the Treasurer of Arapahoe County, Colorado, issued tax certificates on delinquent property in sizes as small as a vigitillionth of the parcel in arrears. The amount of land sometimes conveyed was so small a fractional part of the entire plot that the tax-buyer could not even walk along the strip he had bought without trespassing.

The County Treasurer, D. W. Hart, certified that the sale of the real estate was "for delinquent taxes for the year 1891," and that the purchaser had "paid the respective sum of money set opposite said tract, being the amount of taxes on the whole of said estate."

On October 10, 1892, a vigitillionth share in twenty-three separate tracts located near Littleton, Colorado, was purchased by W. T. Lambert at a minimum cost of 45 cents a share. A similar interest in twenty-four other lots was bought by H. W. Jones, on October 15, 1892. The final redemption was paid thirty-five years later.[17]

W. T. LAMBERT.

Land No. 12955

TREASURER'S
Certificate of Purchase
ARAPAHOE COUNTY.

1891 Tax

STATE OF COLORADO }
COUNTY OF ADAMS }

I hereby certify that this instrument was filed for
record in my office at 8 o'clock A. M.

Dec 30 1909, and is duly
recorded in Book _____ Page No. _____

C. E. _____
Recorder.

By L. H. _____
Deputy.

Fees, $ 10

10¢

The Star Land & Securities Co.
819 Kittredge Bldg, Denver Co.

119

SOURCES

Chapter 7

1. Case and Comment, Vol. 42, No. 1 (Spring), 1936.

2. Deed Book, Vol. 7, p. 25, Sullivan County. Recorder's Office, Laporte, Pennsylvania.

3. Deed Record 47, p. 425, Daviess County, Recorder's Office, Washington, Indiana.

4. American Bar Association Journal (June, 1939), p. 477, et seq., by Allen L. Chickering, Member, San Francisco Bar.

5. Lease Book No. 2, p. 141, Hamilton County. Recorder's Office, Cincinnati, Ohio.

6. Original Steel Check in Office of Lincoln Electric Company, Cleveland, Ohio.

7. Original Shingle Check with Alabama Power Company.

8. Original Shirt-Front Check with Proprietor of Star Palace Laundry, Rochester, N. Y.

9. 2 Ohio Law Reporter 510.

10. Old Time Punishments, by Wm. Andrews, pp. 218-21.

11. A Panorama of the World's Legal Systems, by John H. Wigmore, Vol. II, p. 570.

12. Deed Book F., p. 280, Office of the Recorder of Deeds of Northumberland County, Sunbury, Pennsylvania.

13. Office of Clerk, Fulton County, Lewiston, Illinois.

14. Office of the Secretary of State, Springfield, Illinois. Corporation Department.

15. Clerk's Office, Chautauqua County, New York.

16. Filed in District Court of Iowa, Sioux County, 1915, Case No. 6269, entitled *Jacob DeVries* v. *Chicago & Northwestern Railway Co.*

17. Clerk's Office, Arapahoe County, Littleton, Colorado.

CHAPTER 8

FREAK WILLS

So we'll send round the wine and a bright bumper fill
To the jolly Testator who makes his own will.
                              —*Songs and Verses*, by Neaves

WILLS ordinarily reflect the characters of their makers. They also throw light on the customs and manners of the times in which they were written. The eccentricities of people are usually revealed in such instruments, and it has been the author's good fortune to come across many curious ones.

A will may be either a man's monument or his folly. For the most part, foolish last wills and testaments are the work of sick or aged people who postpone this needful act until the last. Concerning this, his Lordship, Chief Justice Edward Coke, said three centuries ago:

"Few men pinched with the messenger of death, have a disposing memory. Such a will is sometimes in haste and commonly by slender advise and is subject to so many questions in this eagle-eyed world. I find great doubts and controversies daily arise on devises made by last wills, in respect of obscure and insensible words and repugnant sentences, the will being made in haste and some pretend that the

121

testator in respect of extreme pain was *non compos mentis* and divers scruples and questions are moved upon wills. Wills and the construction of them, do more to perplex a man than any other learning; and to make a certain construction of them exceedeth *jurisprudentum artem.*"

REVENGE IN A WILL[1]

ESTATE WILLED TO LORD JESUS

A will filed only thirty years ago in Worcester, Massachusetts, left a fifty-thousand-dollar estate to "Lord Jesus." Charles Hastings of Ashburnham was the testator of this unusual instrument, explaining that he was devising his garden lots and buildings to Jesus, because He was the rightful owner of all lands, according to the Bible (which in his opinion was the first Book of Laws). Mr. Hastings drafted the will twenty-five years before he died and, in conveying the property in consideration of the love and good will of the Lord, he reserved the right to use the lands for life, and to improve and repair the houses and to pay taxes and insurance. This unique will was contested in 1897 by the decedent's heirs, who were successful in having the instrument declared invalid.[2]

Testamentary dispositions of property in some form are of very ancient origin. A forty-five-hundred-year-old will was unearthed some years ago at Kahun, Egypt, by the famous English Egyptologist, William F. Petrie. The ancient document is said to antedate all other known written wills by nearly two thousand years. In describing this oldest written will ever found, dated 2550 B.C., that excellent authority, the *Irish Law Times*, says:

"The document is so curiously modern in form that it might almost be granted probate today. But, in any case, it may be assumed that it marks one of the earliest epochs of legal history, and curiously illustrates the continuity of legal methods. The value, socially, legally and historically, of a will that dates back to patriarchal times is evident."

123

It has been said by reliable sources that "there exists a very curious and ancient testament of Job" which was unearthed and published by Cardinal Mai one hundred years ago. In it reference is made to Job's faithful wife and the time when she was poverty-stricken and forced to sell her hair so as to have bread for her husband. "Many details," says Virgil M. Harris, lawyer-author of *Ancient, Curious and Famous Wills*, "are found there which we may look for in vain in the Canonical Book."[3]

ROMAN VIEWS ON WILLS

Whenever a Roman citizen died without a will, he was regarded in the eyes of the law as still living. This was known in Roman law as the theory of a man's existence after death in the person of his heir. Thus anyone who died intestate in ancient Rome continued to live on in his descendants.

The authority for this queer principle of law was the celebrated legal historian, Sir Henry Sumner Maine. In his famous *Ancient Law*, he said:[4]

"With the Romans it seemed an equally simple and natural process, to eliminate the fact of death from the devolution of rights and obligations. *The testator lived on in his heirs or in the group of his co-heirs.* He was in law the same person with them, and if anyone in his testamentary dispositions had even constructively violated the principle which united his actual and his posthumous existence, the law rejected the defective instrument, and gave the inheritance to the kindred in blood, whose capacity to fulfill the conditions of heirship was conferred on them by the law itself and not by any document which by possibility might be erroneously framed.

"When a Roman citizen died intestate, or leaving no valid will, his descendants or kindred became his heirs according to a scale which will be presently described. The person or class of persons who succeeded did not simply *represent* the deceased, but, in conformity with the theory just delineated, they *continued* his civil life, his legal existence. . . . This indeed is the proper moment for suggesting a doubt which will press on us with greater force the further we plumb the depths of this subject—whether wills would ever have come into being at all if it had not been for these remarkable ideas connected with universal succession. . . . But to the Romans belongs preeminently the credit of inventing the will, the institution which, next to the contract, has exercised the greatest influence in transforming human society."

By this same reasoning all Roman women legally remained children. They never grew up.

On file in the Registry of Wills of Somerset House, London, are the original wills of many great Englishmen, including Dr. Johnson, Lord Nelson, William Pitt, painter Vandyck, Izaak Walton, the Duke of Wellington and William Shakespeare (whose three folio pages are placed under an air-tight frame). For many years the will of Napoleon was to be seen at old Doctors' Commons, until it was restored to France pursuant to Emperor Louis Napoleon's request.

Although neither Lincoln nor Grant left wills, many famous Americans did; some of whom were John Quincy Adams, Captain John Alden, Benedict Arnold, Phineas Taylor Barnum, Henry Ward Beecher, James G. Blaine, Edwin T. Booth, Aaron Burr, Salmon P. Chase, Henry Clay, Jefferson Davis, Stephen A. Douglas, Ralph Waldo Emerson, Grover Cleveland, Benjamin Franklin, Jay Gould, Horace Greeley, Alexander Hamilton, Edward H. Harriman, Patrick Henry, Oliver Wendell Holmes, Washington Irving, Andrew Jackson, Thomas Jefferson, Robert E. Lee, Paul Revere, John Sherman, Myles Standish, Harriet Beecher Stowe, George Washington, Daniel Webster, John Whittier, Brigham Young, James Polk, Gouverneur Morris, James Monroe, Chief Justice Marshall, James Madison, William McKinley, Henry Wadsworth Longfellow, and Samuel L. Clemens (Mark Twain).

James Smithson, an Englishman who never visited the United States, willed a half-million dollars to found the Smithsonian Institute in Washington "for the increase and diffusion of knowledge among men," provided one of his nephews died without issue, legitimate or illegitimate. After ten years of debate in Congress, the Smithson trust fund was finally accepted.[5]

Last Will and Testament

I, Jno. Morgan _____ of the City of London of England _____, being of full age and sound mind and memory, do make, publish and declare this to be my **Last Will and Testament** hereby revoking and annulling all Will or Wills by me heretofore made.

ITEM 1. that all my just debts and funeral expenses be paid out of my estate as soon as possible after my decease.

I further direct my executors to cause some parts of my stomach to be converted into fiddle-strings, and that others should be sublimed into smelling salts, and that the remainder of my body be vitrified into lenses — for optical purposes.

In Witness Whereof, I have hereunto set my hand *J Morgan* in the year of our Lord, 1838

The world may think this to be done in spirit of singularity or whim — but I have a mortal aversion to funeral pomp — and I wish my body to be converted into useful purposes.

ECCENTRICITY V. INSANITY

The English will illustrated presents one of the most outstanding cases of eccentricity on record. A British Court (his Lordship Sir Herbert Jenner Fust) declared the instrument to be valid and adjudged the testator to be sane for the reason that during his lifetime he conducted his affairs with great shrewdness and ability. Judge Redfield's monumental work on wills cites this case as authority distinguishing eccentricity from insanity.[6]

When Jeremy Bentham, the famous English philosopher and writer, died in 1832, he willed his body to Dr. Southward Smith, directing him to preserve his corpse so that it might be placed in a chair at the banquet table where the trustees of the University College Hospital met. Bentham, in turn, bequeathed his entire fortune to the London Hospital—so long as his remains presided at all board meetings. This singular request was faithfully carried out. Dr. Smith wrote:

"Jeremy Bentham left by will his body to me for dissection. I was also to deliver a public lecture over it to medical students and the public generally. The latter I did at Well Street School. After the usual anatomical demonstration, a skeleton was made of the bones. I endeavored to preserve the head untouched, merely drawing away the fluids by placing it under an air-pump over sulphuric acid. By this means the head was rendered as hard as the skulls of the New Zealanders, but all expression was gone, of course. Seeing this would not do for exhibition, I had a model made in wax by a distinguished French artist. I then had the skeleton stuffed out to fit Bentham's own clothes and this wax likeness fitted to the trunk. The whole was then enclosed in a mahogany case with folding glass doors, seated in his armchair and holding in his hand his favorite walking stick, and for some years it remained in a room of my house in Finsbury Square. But I ultimately gave it to University College."

This peculiar testamentary demand was obeyed until 1924. For ninety-two years, the preserved figure of Bentham attended every board meeting of the hospital. Dressed in the philosopher's clothes, wearing a gray, broad-brimmed hat, and with the skull under glass between the feet, sat the lifelike dummy, always present but never voting.[7]

WHITE LINEN CLOTHES

In 1900, an old German professor provided in his will, which was filed for probate in Berlin, that his sole surviving heir (for whom he entertained an intense dislike) should get his estate only on condition that "he should always wear white linen clothes at all seasons of the year, and should not supplement them in winter by extra undergarments."[8]

FLORAL RENTALS

In the proceedings of the Lancaster County Historical Association, under date of September 4, 1896, reference is made to Baron Heinrich Wilhelm Stiegel, well-known Philadelphia iron and glass-works tycoon, who devised the lot on which the Lutheran church now stands in Manheim, Pennsylvania.

The Baron was born in Baden, Germany, in 1730. When

he was twenty, he came to the United States, bringing with him his family's fortune amounting to $200,000. He settled in Philadelphia and proceeded to establish a prosperous glass and iron works there.

In the seventies, Baron Stiegel built a large home in Manheim, Lancaster County, and bequeathed to the old Lutheran church there the real estate on which the present church now stands, for a consideration of five shillings and

"the annual rental of one red rose in the month of June forever."

The annual ceremony has caused great public interest. On the first Sunday in June the payment of the rose takes place. The officers of the church bear the rose to the altar on a costly tray. Amid a large congregation, one of the descendants of the Baron comes forward at the minister's request and receives the rose, accepting it in full payment of all yearly rental then due the Stiegel family from the Lutheran Church.[9]

A similar rental provision was found in a will left by a native of Michigan who devised land to his home town for park purposes, for a rental of "one clover blossom per annum" to be picked on the premises and delivered to his heirs and descendants.[10]

DISSENT

An old resident of Pottsville, Pennsylvania, filed an instrument in 1910 which conveyed land for the erection of a new church on condition that when the church was erected, a certain pastor should be forever barred from preaching any sermons therein.[11]

Another queer will, described by Joseph E. Bright in his book, *To Will or Not to Will*, was one left by "a Scotch dissenting minister who bequeathed a sum of money to his chapel at St. Ives to provide: 'Six Bibles every year, for which six men and six women are to throw dice on Whit Tuesday after the morning service, the minister kneeling the while at the south end of the Communion Table, and praying God to direct the luck to His Glory.' "[12]

DRINK THE SEA

When Julian Micklefield died in 1861, he left a will setting forth his beliefs on prohibition and bequeathing his property to the one who could drink all of the water in the sea. Due to impossibility of performance, the instrument was declared void, the English Court holding that his will was "of an exaggerated visionary nature and incapable of fulfilment."[13]

LAST WILL AND TESTAMENT

In the name of God—Amen.

I, William Shakespeare of Stratford upon Avon in the countie of warr. gent, in perfect health and memorie, God be prayed, doe make and ordayne this my last will and testament—That ys to say:

"I give unto my wief my second best bed with the furniture." * * *

By me,
Wm. SHAKESPEARE
Registered in Doctors' Commons[14]

March 25, 1616.

James William (Hindoo) Graham, an Englishman who had lived in the Near East many years, left a will in 1849 containing provision for the erection of a cenotaph at Constantinople inscribed with his name and bearing a light *forever burning*. The will was upheld by the Judicial Committee of the Privy Council, thereby reversing the ruling of the Prerogative Court which had refused to probate the will "upon the ground of the extraordinary nature of the bequest, coupled with the wild and extravagant conduct of the testator about the time of execution."[15]

INTENTIONALLY

During the reign of William III, an English lawyer by the name of Sergeant Maynard left a will purposely worded in obscure terms so as to give rise to litigation and settle some fine legal points which had arisen and vexed him during lifetime.[16]

NO FUNERAL BELL

In 1840, the will of an Englishman by the name of Zimmerman was probated. It provided:

"No person is to attend my corpse to the grave nor is any funeral bell to be rung; and my desire is to be buried plainly and in a decent manner; and if this be not done, I will come again—that is to say, if I can."[17]

ABOVE GROUND

The strangest annuity on record involved an English army officer in the East India Company's service who died at the turn of the twentieth century in a dilapidated, dingy old house on Ham Street in Ham Common, London. To the officer's wife had been bequeathed a life annuity which was to "be paid as long as she was above ground." When she died, in 1880, her husband refused to forfeit the income by putting her below the ground; and for thirty years was reported to have kept her remains, encased in glass, in a room allotted "to her sole and separate use," thus prolonging enjoyment, if not of his wife's society, at least of her income.[18]

133

POETIC WILL

Private Stanley Frederic Woodburn of Seacombe, Wallasey, Cheshire, a soldier in the Liverpool Regiment, was killed in France during the First World War. He wrote his will in verse two months before his death, on a field service form about the size of a postcard. The will reads:

"My belongings I leave to my next of kin,
My purse is empty, there's nothing in;
My uniform, rifle, my pack and kit,
I leave to the next poor devil 'twill fit;
But if this war I manage to clear
I'll keep it myself for the souvenir."[19]

A BEQUEATHED DINNER

Samuel Jeffery, a sailor on His British Majesty's ship "Amphion," wrote a peculiar testament. It was:

134

"To my friends Jack Dalling, Joe Cape and Tom Board-man—I direct they be given the sum of £10 between them, to pay for a good dinner, which I wish them to have in remembrance of me and request they will drink a speedy and safe passage to me to the other world."[20]

NOT A FARTHING IF THEY MARRIED

General Hawley drew up his own will "because of the hatred and suspicion" with which he regarded all lawyers. He left £100 to a maid by the name of Elizabeth Buskett and the balance of his fortune to his adopted son; but provided that if the two should marry each other, "neither was to inherit a farthing."[21]

CYNICAL PROVISIONS

Many testators leave behind them cynical provisions. Some of the most cryptic have been left by Englishmen and Frenchmen.

In 1847, the cynical Marquis d'Aligré left the following will:

"I leave to my relatives, oblivion;
to my friends, ingratitude;
to God, my soul."[22]

The Earl of Pembroke contributed to the sarcasm already found in last wills and testaments by saying:

"I bequeath to Thomas May, whose nose I did break at a masquerade, 5 shillings. My intention had been to give more, but all who have seen his history of Parliament will consider that even this sum is too large.

"I give to Lieutenant General Cromwell one of my words, the which he must want, seeing that he hath never kept any of his own."[23]

The will left by the famous French satirist, Rabelais, will be long remembered. It ran:

"I have no available property,
I owe a great deal;
The rest I give to the poor."[24]

TO A CLEAN-SHAVEN SON

In 1862, Henry Budd bequeathed his property only to "a clean-shaven son." The singular will contained the following terms:

"In case my son Edward shall wear mustaches, then the devise to him of my estate called Pepper Park shall be void; and I devise the same estate to my son William but in case he shall wear mustaches, then the devise hereinbefore contained in favor of him, his appointees, heirs and assigns of my said estate called Twickenham Park, shall be void."[25]

WILLED TO THE DEAD

Virgil M. Harris, Esq., of the St. Louis Bar, referred in 1911 to a case in which property was willed to the Devil, stating that "a few years ago, a queer old native of that country (Finland) devised all his property to the Devil without attempting to establish the identity of the devisee. The Devil's claim was disregarded and the property went to the heirs of the testator."[26]

SUSPENSE

M. Zalesky of Poland died fifty years ago, leaving property valued at 100,000 roubles. His will was enclosed in an envelope directing it to be opened after death. Inside there was another envelope, "To be opened six weeks after death." When that time elapsed the second envelope was opened and a third one found, "To be opened one year after death." A fourth was discovered at the end of the year, "To be opened two years later"; and so it went on until 1894, when the actual will was discovered and read.[27]

THE PLEDGES OF JOHN HEDGES

In 1737, an eccentric Englishman by the name of John Hedges filed this poetic will in Doctors' Commons:

> "The fifth day of May
> Being airy and gay
> And to Hyp not inclined
> But of vigorous mind
> And my body in health
> I'll dispose of my wealth.
> And I'm to leave
> On this side the grave
> To some one or other
> And I think to my brother
> Because I foresaw

That my brethren-in-law
If I did not take care
Would come in for their share
Which I no-wise intended
Till their manners are mended
And of that God knows, there's no sign.
I do therefore enjoin
And do strictly command
Of which witness my hand
That naught I have got
Be brot into hotch-pot
But I give and devise
As much as in me lies
To the son of my mother
My own dear brother
To have and to hold
All my silver and gold
As the affectionate pledges
Of his brother John Hedges.

ANIMAL BENEFICIARIES

In discussing testamentary capacity, most legal writers agree that a testator is not necessarily insane just because he makes a pet animal the sole beneficiary of his estate. "This strange fondness for animals, in solitary females," said John Proffatt, "is not altogether unusual. In June, 1828, the London papers recorded the singular will of a testator named Garland, containing the following clause: I bequeath to my monkey, my dear and amusing Jacko, the sum of £ 10 sterling per anum, to be employed for his sole use and benefit; to my faithful dog Shock, and my well-beloved cat Tib, a pension of £ 5 sterling; and I desire that, in case of the death of either of the three, the lapsed pension shall pass to the other two, between whom it is to be equally divided. On the death of all three, the sum appropriated to this purpose shall become the property of my daughter Gertrude, to whom I give a preference among my children, because of the large family she has, and the difficulty she finds in bringing them up."

THIRTY SOUS TO CATS

In 1677, Madame Dupuis, also known as Mademoiselle Jeanne Felix, a famous French musician, died; leaving the following will which subsequently was declared void:

"I pray Mademoiselle Bluteau, my sister, and Madame Calogne, my niece, to take care of my cats. Whilst these two live, they shall have 30 sous a month, that they may be well fed. They must have twice a day, meat soup of the quality usually served on table; but they must be given it separately, each having his own saucer. The bread must not be crumbled in the soup, but cut up into pieces about the size of hazel nuts, or they cannot eat it. When boiled beef is put into the pot with the soaked bread, some thin slices of raw meat must be put in as well, and the whole stewed till it is fit for eating. When only one cat lives, half the money will suffice. Nicole Pigeon shall take care of the cats and cherish them. Madame Calogne may go and see them."[28]

A LIBELOUS WILL

A strange will which provoked a suit for libel was recorded in an English work of the highest merit. It was probated in 1781 and read as follows:

"I, John Hylett Stow, hereby direct my executors to lay out five guineas in the purchase of a picture of the viper biting the benevolent hand of the person who saved him from perishing in the snow, if the same can be bought for the money; and that they do in memory of me, present it to a King's counsel, whereby he may have frequent opportunities of contemplating it, and, by a comparison between that and his own virtue, be able to form a certain judgment which is best and most profitable, a grateful remembrance of past friendship and almost parental regard, or ingratitude and insolence. This I direct to be presented to him in lieu of a legacy of three thousand pounds I had by a former will, now revoked and burned, left him."[29]

PETTICOAT WILL

One of the oddest documents ever introduced in a court of law was a woman's petticoat on which was written the will of an eccentric Californian. This case is described by Joseph E. Bright in his book, *To Will or Not to Will*. It was established that the testator had become too weak to write, and not being able to find any paper, one of the two nurses attending wrote his will on her petticoat. It was shown that the wealthy decedent signed the petticoat will by making a cross which was witnessed by the nurses. However, as it was not known until a few months after death that the testator had left an estate, the petticoat bearing the will was hung up unwashed in a closet, completely forgotten. Upon learning that a sizable fortune had been left, one of the nurses remembered the incident and produced the petticoat.

A California jury decided that the will written on the undergarment was authentic and genuine, thereby invalidating an earlier will held by a certain bank. The provisions of the petticoat will directed the bulk of the estate to go to a certain heir of the testator, the two nurses to receive ten thousand dollars apiece, for serving him during his last illness, but since the nurses had served as witnesses on this strange document, they were precluded as a matter of law from participating as beneficiaries in the estate.[30]

WILLS ON ECCENTRIC MATERIALS

Having learned that it makes no difference whether a will is written on paper, parchment, canvas, or wood, just so long as the proper formalities required by the law of wills are complied with, an eccentric testator proceeded to write his last will and testament on a door, and "the executors had no choice but to have it unscrewed from its hinges and carried into court for probate."[31]

An empty eggshell was probated in England during the First World War. A British air pilot by the name of J. Barnes chose that singular object upon which to leave his last will and testament. He wrote:

"To May—Everything I possess. J. B."

"In England a recluse wrote his will, while too weak to contact human aid, upon the corner of a bedpost," says Joseph E. Bright, in *To Will or Not to Will*.[32]

He also tells about a will which was written on a matchbox and offered for probate in California.[33] Robert J. McElroy of Pittsburgh scribbled his will on a card torn from a freight car, after being fatally injured by a freight train. On this strange document, which was filed in 1910 as a will in Pittsburgh, McElroy had written:

"Mary, all that is mine is thine."[34]

Joseph Dwyer of Weymouth, Massachusetts, left a $50,000 estate to his wife by writing his will on a piece of grocer's brown wrapping paper. The will was probated in the Norfolk County Court at Dedham (October, 1910) and subsequently declared valid.[35]

Nicholas Zinner wrote his will on the lid of a collar box while enroute to the United States in 1910 on the S. S. "Kaiser Wilhelm der Grosse," bequeathing $700 cash and $10,000 in securities to his wife. After the testator jumped overboard, government officials searched Zinner's cabin and found the will, forwarding it to Frau Zinner.[36]

Sailor Ed McCall of Asheville, N. C., tattooed a will on a man's back in the presence of his attorney who witnessed the actual signing. Upon death, if the flesh bearing the tattoo marks constituting the will is severed from the corpse and preserved, many authorities assert that it can be validly probated, provided all formal requisites were adhered to at the time the unique will was made.

A will was tattooed on the back of a very beautiful young lady, according to Rider Haggard; but his source in *Mr. Meeson's Will* reveals the story to be entirely legend.[37] The case centered around a wealthy but cruel publisher who disinherited his nephew and later found himself shipwrecked on a desert island with his nephew's sweetheart. Eventually seeing the errors of his ways, the publisher begged to set things right by willing his property to his nephew. Not finding any writing materials available on the island, the old man prevailed upon a sailor to tattoo the will across the girl's shoulders. When the strange will was completed, the testator made his mark.

The famous legal periodical, *Green Bag*, recounts:

"Of course she was rescued by a passing vessel, rejoined her lover and sought to establish his rights. For this purpose the will had to be probated and the law required the original will to be filed in the office. But the registrar, touched by 'beauty in distress' allowed a photograph of the will to be filed. The will was contested by the heirs, but after an exciting trial, described at length in the story, victory perched on the shoulders of the lady, who later married the nephew-beneficiary and lived happily ever after."

The most beautiful will ever written was conceived by the late Williston Fish of the Chicago Bar. He wrote it in 1897. It first appeared in *Harper's Weekly* in 1898 and since then has been republished many hundreds of times in newspapers and magazines. It has been translated into many foreign languages, and numerous times the testator, Charles Lounsbury, has been erroneously pictured as an insane Chicago lawyer who died in the Cook County Asylum at Dunning, Illinois.

A copy of this "classic of wills" reads as follows:

IN THE NAME OF GOD, AMEN.

I, Charles Lounsbury, being of sound and disposing mind and memory (he lingered on the word memory), do now make and publish this my last will and testament, in order, as justly as I may, to distribute my interests in the world among succeeding men.

And first, that part of my interests which is known among men and recognized in the sheep-bound volumes of the law as my property, being inconsiderable and of none-account, I make no account of in this my will.

My right to live, it being but a life estate, is not at my disposal, but these things excepted, all else in the world I now proceed to devise and bequeath.

Item—And first, I give to good fathers and mothers, but in trust for their children, nevertheless, all good little words of praise and all quaint pet names, and I charge said parents to use them justly but generously as the needs of their children shall require.

Item—I leave to children exclusively, but only for the life of their childhood, all and every the dandelions of the fields and the daisies thereof, with the right to play among them freely, according to the custom of children, warning them at the same time against the thistles. And I devise to children the yellow shores of creeks and the golden sands beneath the waters thereof, with the dragon flies that skim the surface of said waters, and the odors of the willows that dip into said waters, and the white clouds that float high over the giant trees.

And I leave to children the long, long days to be merry in, in a thousand ways, and the Night and the Moon and the train of the Milky Way to wonder at, but subject, nevertheless, to the rights hereinafter given to lovers; and I give to each child the right to choose a star that shall be his, and I direct that the child's father shall tell him the name of it, in order that the child shall always remember the name of that star after he has learned and forgotten astronomy.

Item—I devise to boys jointly all the useful idle fields and commons where ball may be played, and all snow-clad hills where one may coast, and all streams and ponds where one may skate, to have and to hold the same for the period of their boyhood. And all meadows, with the clover blooms and butterflies thereof; and all woods, with their appurtenances of squirrels and whirring birds and echoes and strange noises; and all distant places which may be visited, together with the adventures there found, I do give to said boys to be theirs. And I give to said boys each his own place at the fireside at night, with all pictures that may be seen in the burning wood or coal, to enjoy without let or hindrance and without any incumbrance of cares.

Item—To lovers I devise their imaginary world, with whatever they may need, as the stars of the sky, the red, red roses

145

by the wall, the snow of the hawthorn, the sweet strains of music, or aught else they may desire to figure to each other the lastingness and beauty of their love.

Item—To young men jointly, being joined in a brave, mad crowd, I devise and bequeath all boisterous, inspiring sports of rivalry. I give to them the disdain of weakness and un-daunted confidence in their own strength. Though they are rude and rough, I leave to them alone the power of making lasting friendships and of possessing companions and to them exclusively I give all merry songs and brave choruses to sing, with smooth voices to troll them forth.

Item—And to those who are no longer children or youths or lovers I leave Memory, and I leave to them the volumes of the poems of Burns and Shakespeare, and of other poets, if there are others, to the end that they may live the old days over again freely and fully, without tithe or diminution; and to those who are no longer children or youths or lovers I leave, too, the knowledge of what a rare, rare world it is.[38]

A DEFIANT WILL

In contrast to the world's most beautiful will, there is the testament left in 1800 by Captain Blackhouse who was buried in an *upright* coffin in Buckinghamshire. He left the follow-ing directions:

"I will have nothing to do with the church or the church-yard: bury me in my own wood on the hill, and my sword with me, and I'll defy all the evil spirits in existence to injure me."[39]

NO FUNERAL EXPENSE

Eighty-six years later Judge J. R. Ludlow of Pittsburgh left these practical testamentary directions:

"I request my executors to incur at my funeral no expense not absolutely required. My estate is small, and my wife and children ought to have every dollar for their support. Let no false pride dictate ostentatious display, for after the soul departs from the body, it matters little what becomes of that body, so that it is decently buried. God will protect the dust."[40]

A SMOKER'S WILL

M. Klaes of Rotterdam amassed a large fortune in the linen trade during the latter part of the last century. His hobby was collecting pipes, and during his eighty years he smoked over four tons of tobacco and consumed a half-million quarts of beer. Just before he died, he made his will, in which he invited all smokers of the country to attend his funeral and receive two pipes and ten pounds of tobacco, for smoking during his funeral services. Finally, he directed that his casket "be lined with the cedar of his old Havana cigar

147

boxes, and that a box of old Dutch tobacco should be placed at the foot of his coffin; his favorite pipe and a box of matches at his side, 'as one does not know what might happen.' "[41]

A GUARDED BEARD

When Lincoln was a candidate for the presidency, Valentine Tapley of Pike County, Missouri, a dyed-in-the-wool Democrat, vowed that if Lincoln was elected, he would never cut his beard. When Mr. Tapley died in 1910 he was eighty years old. He had taken great pride in his whiskers, which measured twelve and a half feet; and due to fear that his grave would be robbed for his unusually long whiskers, he provided in his will for a tomb of double strength to guard against such an exigency.[42]

One of the strangest wills ever drawn by a lawyer was one that was filed for probate in LeMars, Iowa, on September 15, 1930. T. M. Zink, a wealthy Iowa attorney, left a will which disinherited his wife and two daughters and provided for a fund of $50,000 to build a "womanless library" at LeMars. The bequest was to be lent at interest for seventy-five years, at the end of which time the lawyer-testator figured over four million dollars would have accumulated. This amount was then to endow a library which he described as follows:

"No woman shall at any time, under any pretense or for any purpose, be allowed inside the library, or upon the premises or have any say about anything concerned therewith, nor appoint any person or persons to perform any act connected therewith. No book, work of art, chart, magazine, picture, unless some production by a man, shall be allowed inside or outside the building, or upon the premises, and this shall include all decorations for inside and outside of the building. *There shall be over each entrance to the premises and building, a sign in these words:* 'NO WOMAN ADMITTED.' It is my intention to forever exclude all women from the premises and having anything to say or do with the trust estate and library. . . . If any woman, or women shall be allowed to disregard any of the limitations herein placed upon them, it shall be ground for removal of the trust estate and library, from where located. . . . My intense hatred of women is not of recent origin or development nor based upon any personal differences I ever had with them but is the result of my experiences with women, observations of them, and study of all literatures and philosophical works, within my limited knowledge relating thereto."

One of the heirs contested the will in 1931 and the Plymouth District Court of Iowa broke the will and divided the estate among the lawful heirs.[43]

YORICK'S SKULL

For forty-four years John Reed served as gaslighter of the Walnut Street Theater in Philadelphia, without missing a single performance. Unable to act on the stage while alive, he carried out after death a secret ambition to assume a role in one of Shakespeare's plays, by providing a clause in his will which read as follows:

"My head to be separated from my body immediately after death; the latter to be buried in a grave; the former, duly macerated and prepared, to be brought to the theatre, where I have served all my life and to be employed to represent the skull of Yorick—and to this end I bequeath my head to the properties."[44]

PRESERVED SKULLS

The skull of Cartouche, the famous French bandit, can still be seen in the library of the Genovevan monastery at Paris. Cartouche himself asked, while being tortured to death on the wheel, that his skull be so preserved.[45]

In York Castle one finds the skull of Eugene Aaram, who bequeathed it for display purposes only.

Professor Morlet of Lausanne, Switzerland, wanted his head to be sent to the Berne Anatomical Museum, and to make certain they would get his skull and no other, he directed his name to be distinctly engraven on it.

PRESERVED ORGANS

In February, 1827, an Englishman by the name of Dr. Ellerby died, bequeathing his heart, lungs and brains to various named friends. Some of the rare clauses in his will follow:

"Item: I desire that immediately after my death my body shall be carried to the Anatomical Museum in Alderside Street, and shall be there dissected by Drs. Lawrence, Tyrell, and Wardrup, in order that the cause of my malady may be well understood.

"Item: I bequeath my heart to Mr. W. an anatomist; my lungs to Mr. R.; and my brains to Mr. F. in order that they may preserve them from decomposition; and I declare that if these gentlemen shall fail faithfully to execute these my last wishes in this respect I will come—if it should be by any means possible—and torment them until they shall comply."[46]

DRUMHEADS

According to Bright's *To Will or Not to Will*, "At the end of the Revolutionary War one testator left his body to the anatomical museum of Harvard, with the gruesome provision that two drumheads were to be made of his skin. Upon one was to be inscribed Alexander Pope's 'Universal Prayer,' and on the other the 'Declaration of Independence'; and then they were to be presented to the testator's distinguished friend, the drummer of Cohasset. This presentation was subject to the condition that on the 17th of June at sunrise, every year, the drummer should beat 'on the drumheads at the foot of Bunker Hill the spirit-stirring strains of *Yankee Doodle*.' "[47]

AN IDOL HEIR

A resident of India provided by will some four hundred years ago that his property should pass to the use of a certain idol. In 1900 one of the heirs of the original testator left a will devising the same property to somebody else; but the Judiciary Committee of the Privy Council of Great Britain refused to recognize the subsequent will, declaring the original devise to the idol to be valid. Mr. Justice Riddell of the Supreme Court of Canada unearthed this remarkable oddity.[48]

152

In 1939, the will of the late chief counsel for the Goodyear Tire & Rubber Company was filed in Akron, Ohio, asking the court

"not to permit apparently reputable lawyers and administrators to fleece the legatees as they do each day" and forbade the appointment of a trust company as administrator on account of his "unfortunate experiences with so-called trust companies as institutions wholly incompetent to transact the business they claim superiority in."[49]

Apparently the only way to avoid pitfalls is to die poor.

A WILL IN SHORTHAND

According to *English Law Notes*, says the *Ohio Law Reporter*, Vol. 20, page 210, "a will *written in shorthand* was admitted to probate—in February, 1922—the second one of its kind. The judges ordered a certified transcript for use." It was added that "the admission of such wills may prove a great boon to solicitors called on to make a death bed will. . . . In the case of a testator *in extremis* this might save an undesirable intestacy."

PHONOGRAPH-RECORD EVIDENCE

In July, 1908, a phonograph record of the decedent-testator was evidence in a will contest case tried in Vienna. According to a correspondent of the *St. Louis Dispatch:*

"Professor Sulzer stated that he had a phonographic record that would settle beyond question the point in dispute and asked the court's permission to introduce it as evidence. The permission was granted and Mme. Blaci, the decedent, told in her own voice of her affection for her brother and his family and announced her intention of providing before her death so that her nephew, Heinrich, would be well cared for after she had passed away.

"Heinrich testified that the record was made on the twenty-fifth anniversary of his birth. Mme. Blaci, he told the judge, had said at the time that she wanted the words she had spoken to her brother, Heinrich's father, put on record as a souvenir of her affection that could be handed down to her nephew.

"After hearing the record, the court immediately awarded Heinrich $120,000 as his share of the estate, which was the full amount claimed by him."[50]

BALLAD ON WILLS

In concluding a chapter on freak wills, an old English ballad is appropriate:

You had better pay toll when you take to the road,
Than attempt by a by-way to reach your abode;
You had better employ a conveyancer's hand,
Than encounter the risk that your will shouldn't stand.
From the broad beaten track where the traveler strays,
He may land in a bog or be lost in a maze;
And the law, when defied, will avenge itself still,
On the men and the women who make their own will.
—from *The Jolly Testator Who Makes His Own Will*

SOURCES

Chapter 8

1. Surrogate Court of Middlesex County, Woodbridge, N. J.
2. Probate Office, Worcester, Mass.

3. Ancient, Curious and Famous Wills, by V. M. Harris, Little, Brown & Co., p. 10.

4. Ancient Law, by Sir Henry Sumner Maine, pp. 156-7.

5. Smithsonian Institute, Washington, D. C.

6. Redfield on Wills, Vol. 1, 2nd Ed., Chap. III, p. 69.

7. Legal Antiquities, by Edward J. White, p. 324.

8. Ancient, Curious and Famous Wills, by V. M. Harris, Little, Brown & Co., p. 159.

9. Proceedings of Lancaster County Historical Association (September 4, 1896).

10. Ancient, Curious and Famous Wills, by V. M. Harris, Little, Brown & Co., p. 232.

11. Recorder's Office, Pottsville, Pa.

12. To Will or Not to Will, by Joseph E. Bright, Dennis & Co., Inc., p. 43. *Morgan v. Boys.*

13. Miscellaneous (1868), Part 4, Sec. 6, Art. 2, by Chas. A. Swinburne.

14. Curiosities and Law of Wills, by John Proffatt, pp. 21, 22, 23.

15. *Austen v. Graham*, 29 Eng. L. & Eq. 38 (1855); 14 Eng. Reprint 188 (1854).

16. Curiosities of Law and Lawyers, p. 491.

17. The Curiosities and Law of Wills, by John Proffatt, Vol. II, p. 10.

18. Ancient, Curious and Famous Wills, by V. M. Harris, Little, Brown & Co., pp. 185, 186.

19. Docket, Vol. 5 (Winter, 1938-39), No. 1, p. 3994.

20. U. S. Law Review.

21. Ancient, Curious and Famous Wills, by V. M. Harris, Little, Brown & Co., p. 167.

22. Ancient, Curious and Famous Wills, by V. M. Harris, Little, Brown & Co., pp. 249-251.

23. Leading in Law and Curious in Court, by Benjamin F. Burnham, pp. 1294-5.

24. Ancient, Curious and Famous Wills, by V. M. Harris, Little, Brown & Co., p. 43.

25. Ancient, Curious and Famous Wills, by V. M. Harris, Little, Brown & Co., p. 87.

26. Ancient, Curious and Famous Wills, by V. M. Harris, Little, Brown & Co., p. 241.

27. Ancient, Curious and Famous Wills, by V. M. Harris, Little, Brown & Co., pp. 182, 183.

28. Curiosities of Olden Times, by S. Baring-Gould, pp. 47, 48.

29. Curiosities of the Search Room.

30. To Will or Not to Will, by Joseph E. Bright, Dennis & Co., Inc., pp. 55, 56.

31. Ancient, Curious and Famous Wills, by V. M. Harris, Little, Brown & Co., pp. 167, 168.

32. To Will or Not to Will, by Joseph E. Bright, Dennis & Co., Inc., p. 55.

33. To Will or Not to Will, by Joseph E. Bright, Dennis & Co., Inc., p. 57.

34. Probate Court, Pittsburgh, Pa.

35. Surrogate Court, Norfolk County, Mass.

36. Ancient, Curious and Famous Wills, by V. M. Harris, Little, Brown & Co., pp. 168, 169.

37. Mr. Meesom's Will, by Rider Haggard.

38. Harper's Weekly (1898).

39. Harper's Weekly, July 5, 1879, Col. 2, p. 530.

40. Leading in Law and Curious in Court, by Benjamin F. Burnham, p. 1349.

41. Ancient, Curious and Famous Wills, by V. M. Harris, Little, Brown & Co., p. 200.

42. Ancient, Curious and Famous Wills, by V. M. Harris, Little, Brown & Co., pp. 155, 156.

43. Office of Clerk of District Court, Plymouth County, Iowa.

44. Ancient, Curious and Famous Wills, by V. M. Harris, Little, Brown & Co., p. 136.

45. Ancient, Curious and Famous Wills, by V. M. Harris, Little, Brown & Co., p. 135.

46. Ancient, Curious and Famous Wills, by V. M. Harris, Little, Brown & Co., pp. 129, 130.

47. To Will or Not to Will, by Joseph E. Bright, Dennis & Co., Inc., p. 33.

48. Mr. Justice Riddell of Supreme Court of Canada.

49. Probate Court, Summit County, Akron, Ohio.

50. Ohio Law Reporter, vol. 6, p. 301.

CHAPTER 9

UNCOMMON LAW

Laws are like cobwebs—
Where the small flies are caught—
But the great break thru.
—Bacon's Apothegms

ALMOST everyone has heard something about the famous common law of England; very few have heard of its *uncommon* law. However, since the dawn of legal history, peculiarities have crept into the law.

SANCTUARIES FOR CRIMINALS

The Church has been a potent influence, especially in creating privileges and immunities.

One of the earliest places of refuge for criminals was the Church; because from the fourteenth to the seventeenth century, in England, an escaping fugitive need only reach the front door of any church and grasp its sanctuary knocker and he was legally free from arrest. One can see on the door of Durham Cathedral the heavy bronze knocker which saved many a criminal from instant death. For in those days, when a fugitive from justice struck the knocker, he claimed what was known in the law as the holy right of sanctuary. He was not asked any questions but only required to leave his weapons at the door. For about forty days he was given food and bed and then, if no pardon had been obtained, he was allowed to escape to another country. Francis Watt, a nineteenth-century legal historian, described how a man took sanctuary in olden days:[1]

"Having stricken (let us say) his fellow, he fled to the cathedral and knocked at the door of the galilee. Over the north porch were two chambers where watchers abode night and day. The minute the door closed behind the fugitive, the galilee bell proclaimed to the town that another life was safe from them that hunted. Then the prior assigned him a gown of black cloth marked on the left shoulder with the yellow cross of St. Cuthbert, and therewith a narrow space where he might lie secure of life, though ill at ease. So it was at Durham. . . . He was fed and lodged in some rough sort for forty days, within which time he must confess his crime before the coroner at the churchyard gate, and so constitute himself the King's felon. Then he swore to abjure the realm. The coroner assigned him a port of embarkatation (chosen by himself), whither he must hasten with bare head, carrying in his hand a cross, not departing, save in direst need, from the King's highway. He might tarry on the shore but a single ebb and flow of the tide, unless it were impossible to come by a ship, in which case he must wade up to his knees in the sea every day. He was thus protected for another forty days, when, if he could not find passage, he returned whence he came, to try his luck elsewhere."

The Cathedral in Durham was the most famous sanctuary in old England. There were many others, however, including the special sanctuaries, which were St. Martin's le Grand

159

and Westminster. The latter served as a shelter against civil process until 1724. For this reason, "taking to Westminster" became a very common phrase among escaping felons.

To this very day one finds in English churches the "frid-stol" chairs carved out of stone which, during the Middle Ages, symbolized to condemned prisoners a haven of immunity; for even a murderer was exempt from punishment when he sat in it. Baedeker refers to the stone chairs of peace in both the Beverly Minster in Beverly and the Abbey Church in Hexham, recalling the fact that these churches once possessed the privilege of inviolable stanctuary.[2]

THE "NECK VERSE"

"Have mercy upon me, O God. According to Thy loving kindness—according unto the multitude of Thy tender mercies—blot out my transgressions."

For centuries, condemned criminals who could read this
verse from the Book of Psalms of the Old Testament saved
themselves from the English gallows. This was called "benefit of clergy." The quotation from the Bible became known
as the "neck verse" because it saved so many necks from the
hangman's noose. Literally thousands of criminals condemned to die were benefited by clergy and permitted to
escape the death sentence by reciting this one passage from
the Scriptures.[3]

This fantastic legal proceeding of escaping penalty by
means of "benefit of clergy" remained on the English statute
books until 1841. It has been vividly described by Francis
Watt, a legal historian of British fame, who said:[4]

"First the privilege was confined to such as had the clerical
dress and tonsure, afterwards it was extended to their assist-
ants, the very doorkeepers being held within the charmed
circle; yet the line had to be drawn somewhere, and how to

161

decide when every ruffian at his wits' end for a defense, was certain with blatant voice to claim the privilege? Well, could he read? If so, ten to one he was an ecclesiastic of some sort, and therefore entitled to his clergy. . . . As regards the reading, it must not be supposed that a difficult examination was passed by the prisoner before he escaped. You had but to read what came to be significantly called the Neck-verse from the book which the officer of court handed you where you 'prayed your clergy.' The Neck-verse was the first verse of the fifty-first Psalm in the Vulgate. It was only three words—*Miserere mei Deus*—'Have mercy on me, O God.' . . .

"A person who claimed clergy was branded on the crown of his thumb with an 'M' if he were a murderer, with a 'T' if he were guilty of any other felony. . . .

"In the reign of James I, women got the benefit of clergy in certain cases, and afterwards they were put on the same footing as men. Then in 1705 the necessity for reading was abolished and in 1779 so was branding."

NO WITNESSES

French was the legal tongue in England for over three hundred and fifty years. During that time no criminal could have any witnesses take the stand to declare his innocence. Such was the fate of an Englishman during the thirteenth and fourteenth centuries.[5]

FAMILY REVENGE

Another peculiar quirk of the English common law was the duty placed upon the kin of a murdered person. From 1409 to the time of Chief Gascoigne—

"the dead man's wife and all of his kin were required to drag the felon to execution."[6]

This one grim piece of archaism remained far into the middle ages to take the original place of tribal or family revenge.

NO COMPLAINT WITHOUT A WITNESS

Another requisite rigidly enforced in England, from 1215 to as late as 1834, was the necessity of corroboration of complaint. Thus, for over six hundred years, no Englishman could make a legal complaint unless he first showed he had a witness.[7] This must have been an offshoot of the Roman law, because for over half a century in Rome a case with only one witness was always thrown out of court.[8]

The ban on women witnesses in ancient Athens was equally absurd. Only in homicide cases were Athenian women legally permitted to serve as witnesses. In all other cases they were denied the privilege.[9]

THE WHOLE TOWN A JUDGE

For several hundred years in England whole towns served as judges in criminal cases.[10] Oftentimes, everyone in the community would set about to apprehend the criminal because of the extreme tax penalty which would be assessed upon the inhabitants if they let him go free.

In those early days, every citizen was deemed an enforcement officer, charged with the duty of investigating, indicting, judging and convicting. How times have changed! Perhaps for the better, perhaps no. Who can say?

TRANSFER OF PROPERTY

Nowadays, title to land is transferred by a piece of paper known as a deed. Such was not the case in years past, for the reason that very few people knew how to read or write. Therefore, manual delivery of a clod of earth, known as "livery of seisen," symbolized a transfer of ownership of real estate. Hence land transfers in England were legally carried out by the mere passing of "turf or twig" for hundreds of years. Title to a house was conveyed by delivering "the hasp of the door."[11]

In Scotland during the fifteenth century, if a dish was broken over a fire, land was legally reconveyed to its original owner. In all probability, this was an offshoot of the Roman custom which recognized the breaking of a straw to mean the sealing of a contract.[12]

Among the Saxons, in order to relinquish all interest in an estate, one need only make a gesture "with curved fingers." This served in place of a document, and the ceremony was legally binding.

The custom of throwing an old shoe after the bride and bridegroom as they leave the church or as they start on their honeymoon is of exceedingly ancient date. It originated with the Jewish law of old which provided that in order validly to pass title to property in land, the original possessor untied his shoe and gave it to the new purchaser or inheritor in token of complete abandonment of all present and future claim. It is said that in early Anglo-Saxon marriages the father of the bride delivered one of her shoes to the bridegroom who touched her head with it. This was done as a symbol of his authority.

JURIES THEN AND NOW

Today if a prospective juror indicates that he witnessed the matter in dispute or "in issue" as it is called, he may be struck off "for cause" and not be permitted to remain on the panel. Such was not the case in former times. Then only those jurors who were acquainted with the facts in dispute were allowed to remain seated in the jury box.[13]

165

A FREE BITE

This was no more extraordinary than the well-known common-law doctrine which entitled every dog in England, during the eighteenth and nineteenth centuries, to a free bite.[14] Not until a dog had bitten a person for the second time did its master have to respond in damages. So it was that Oliver Goldsmith wrote:

"The man recovered of the bite,
The dog it was that died."

166

SOURCES

Chapter 9

1. The Law's Lumber Room, by Francis Watt, pp. 85, 86.
2. Sanctuaries, by William E. Axon, pp. 17-20.
3. Psalms 51:i.
4. The Law's Lumber Room, by Francis Watt, pp. 3, 4, 5, 8.
5. The Story of the Law, by John M. Zane, pp. 279, 281.
6. 13 Harvard Law Review, p. 179.
7. Older Modes of Trial, by Thayer, H. L. R. (2) 46.
8. 15 Harvard Law Review (1901), p. 84.
9. Lawyers and Litigants in Ancient Athens, by R. J. Bonner, p. 55.
10. Early Law and Custom, by Maine, Chap. 6.
11. "On Symbols," Curiosities of Law, by George Neilson, pp. 48, 52.
12. "On Symbols," Curiosities of Law, by George Neilson, p. 57.
13. The Story of the Law, by John M. Zane, p. 276.
14. *Mason* v. *Keeling*, 91 Eng. Reprint (1710), 1305.

CHAPTER 10

ANCIENT METHODS
OF TRIAL

"The charge is prepared, the lawyers are set;
The judges are ranged, a terrible show."
—Beggar's Opera

"TRIAL BY BIER"

ONE UNUSUAL method of trial legally permitted dead men to serve as witnesses in murder cases. In early times, one accused of murder was forced to touch the corpse of the murdered person. If it appeared to move, the accused was found guilty. This was known as "trial by bier"—the bier being the bed upon which the body

lay. The origin of it has been traced back to Denmark during the reign of King Christian the Second; and it is interesting to note that it was founded upon the belief that the body of the murdered man would show signs, by bleeding or movement, when the assassin approached.[1]

"According to one of the picturesque legends of English history," says one legal writer,[2]

"When Richard the Lion-Heart encountered at Fontevrault his father's body, the blood gushed from the nostrils of the dead king, a proceeding which, as Richard's offense was at the most but unkindness, showed a somewhat excessive sensibility on the part of royal clay.

"The oddest and latest case of all is from Scotland. In 1688 Philip Stanfield was tried for parricide at Edinburgh; one count of the indictment stated how his father's body had bled at his sacrilegious touch. The Lord Advocate, Sir George Mackenzie of Rosehough, the 'Bluidy Mackenzie' of covenanting legend and tradition, conducted the prosecution, and philosophic and cultured jurist as he was, he yet dwelt with much emphasis on the portentous sign. There was no lack of more satisfactory, if more commonplace evidence, and young Stanfield assuredly merited the doom in the end meted out to him."

A METHOD FOR CIVIL CASES

Of all the trials known, the endurance contest on a cross seems the most ridiculous. Yet it was employed in many European countries as the legal method of trying civil cases.[3] The church or its grounds served as the place of trial where the judges and all parties assembled. Generally, the young-

169

est and strongest priests participated and stood in the place of the actual parties. However, they had first to be stripped of their robes, since in theory, at least, the church was divorced from this procedure.

Standing on each side of a cross, at a given signal each would stretch out his arms at full length, to form a cross with his body. The man whose representative first lowered his arms or shifted his position lost the case.

Another form of this kind of trial required the accused to be placed before two relics. Two dice were produced, one marked with a cross. The accused was then asked to guess which one had the cross on it. If he chose the right one, he was acquitted; otherwise he was convicted.[4]

OATHS

The cross has been closely identified with the law. In medieval times, it was equivalent to an oath. The custom of placing the sign of a cross on deeds and documents dates back to the tenth century.[5] With or without the name of the person, an "X" mark was regarded as equivalent to an oath and appeared either at the head or the foot of the script. The usage still survives in the attestation mark of those who are illiterate or too weak to execute the signature in full.

Before discussing other ancient modes of trial, it might be interesting to know the reason why a witness raises his right hand before testifying. Back in the olden days, the Lois du Roi required witnesses to extend their right hands so as to signify that they had pledged their hands to tell the truth. If the testimony of a witness was proved false, his right hand was cut off. The custom of *raising* the hand when taking an oath had its origin in these courts of medieval France.

KNIFE TRIALS

During the thirteenth century in Ipswich, England, "knife trials" were commonly employed. According to a reliable authority,[6]

"it was customary for the defendant who denied a debt to bring into court ten men who were divided into two equal groups, between which a knife was thrown, and the five toward whom the handle fell would sit aside, while the other five would remain with him who was to make his law."

COMPURGATION

Another uncommon form of trial was compurgation. If the person sued could furnish twelve witnesses (known as compurgators) who would swear to the best of their belief

171

that the defendant was telling the truth, he would win his lawsuit (as he was regarded in law to have been purged or cleared of the charges).

As was said by Sir Francis Watt, the famous legal historian:[7]

"If a man were charged with (say) theft before either the Hundred or Shire Court, he was tried in a fashion vastly different from that obtaining today. The complainant was sworn on the holy relics: 'By the Lord I accuse not this man either for hatred, or for envy, or for unlawful lust of gain.' This solemn accusation made out a *prima facie* case against the suspect, who instantly rebutted oath with oath: 'By the Lord I am guiltless, both in deed and in counsel of this charge.' When he produced twelve compurgators, who swore by the Lord: 'The oath is clean and unperjured which this man hath sworn'; then the prisoner went free. These compurgators were witnesses to character. Their testimony had no reference to the particular facts of the case; they simply alleged their belief in accused's innocence but 'sometimes their oath burst' (as the curious technical phrase ran), that is, the accused was caught with his booty or he was a stranger of whom nothing was known; or a Welshman whose veracity was never an article of faith; then there was an appeal to the Judicium Dei, and the Creator was called upon to prove beyond dispute the guilt or innocence of the accused."

It was not until 1833 that this procedure was abolished in England (2 and 3 Will. IV, c. 42, par. 13, Act of Parliament), having been employed in the case of *Ring* v. *Williams*, 8 Barn. & Cress, 5387, as late as 1824.

For many hundreds of years, this oath-swearing procedure

was employed in law courts throughout Europe. In Italy, it was used in a clerical court as late as November, 1904.

Before 1268, posthumous oaths of compurgators seem to have been accepted in London, for a charter of Henry III granted citizens the right to "deraign themselves by oath in crown pleas, except that they should not swear on the graves of the dead as to what the deceased would have said when alive."[8]

TRIAL BY HOT WATER

Another older mode of trial is often known as the trial by hot water. During the Middle Ages, if one accused of crime could put his hand in scalding water without burning it, he was let free. The more serious the crime charged, the deeper the hand would have to go in the cauldron. In murder cases, the arm was thrust in up to the shoulder. If the flesh ap-

173

peared burned some three days later, conviction resulted; otherwise acquittal was ordered.[9]

Trial by ordeal was more ancient than the Church itself and one finds traces of it in the Old Testament and in the *Laws of Mann*. Although this procedure was employed for centuries, it was finally supplanted by the jury system. The water ordeal was one of the earliest forms of trial by ordeal, or judgments by God, as they were sometimes called.

An ancient manuscript gives the following description:

"In the ordeal by hot water the accused, by plunging his hand to the wrist in the boiling fluid, brought forth a stone suspended therein by cord. (This was the single ordeal, and it became the triple when the plunge was up to the elbow.) The arm was done up in bandages not to be removed till after three days; if the scald had healed the man was innocent, if it still festered he was guilty. In the ordeal by hot iron, a piece of red-hot metal was carried a distance of nine feet; it was then dropped and the hand was bandaged, as already set forth. A knight had to thrust his fist into a glowing gauntlet; another form was to walk blindfolded with naked feet over a sequence of red-hot ploughshares. We have a picturesque circumstantial and absolutely untrustworthy Monkish account of how Emma, mother of Edward the Confessor, being suspected of an all-too-intimate acquaintance with Alwyn, Bishop of Winchester, underwent this trial. She took nine steps for herself and five for the Bishop, fixing her eyes the while on heaven. 'When shall we reach these ploughshares?' queried she. How agreeable a surprise to find her little promenade already past and done with! No need to swathe *her* feet, the red-hot iron had marked them not at all."[10]

174

THE COLD-WATER TRIAL

There was another type of trial by water. It was known as the cold-water trial, and had its origin in the ninth century, serving as a popular form of deciding legal disputes for many centuries.[11] The accused was bound tightly with cords and lowered by rope into the water. If he floated, he was adjudged guilty, but if he sank, he was pronounced innocent.[12]

In the words of a celebrated legal historian of those times: [13]

"And now, having been stripped, he kissed the Book and the Cross, was sprinkled with holy water and was cast in, to float if he were guilty; to sink if he were not. But there was the rub—how about death by suffocation? Sir James Stephen suggests that it was all a mode of happy despatch. Or (one fancies) it might be an elementary form of the famous verdict 'not guilty, but don't do it again,' with the chance of doing it again effectually provided against. On the other hand, a recipe for immersion in a thirteenth-century manuscript of

175

the Monastery of Becca reduces the proceedings to the level of farce. The hands of the accused were tied, and a rope was put round his waist; 'and let a knot be made in the rope as high up as the longest hair of the man's head will reach, and then in this way let him be gently lowered into the water; and if he sinks down to the knot, let him be pulled out as innocent; if not, let him be adjudged guilty.' How *not* to sink under such conditions."

Women accused of witchery in the United States were forced to stand trial in this peculiar way. The New England "ducking stool" exacting a water penalty for common scolds and gossipers emanated from this unique form of trial. Obviously a good set of lungs was required in order to escape conviction. A submersion of only a few minutes was sufficient for an acquittal. In this cigarette-smoking age, most of us might be declared innocent under this form of trial, but we would not live to know about the verdict.

It is said that the cold-water trial had its origin in Sicily. When the oath of a witness was doubted, it was scribbled on a board and thrown down a certain well in Siracusa. If it floated, it meant the witness was telling the truth. If it sank, it meant he had been guilty of perjury.

TRIAL BY COMBAT

Another legal form of appeal to the judgment of God was trial by wager of battle.[14] The origin of this custom cannot be traced, for it was found existent almost everywhere in Europe at the dawn of legal history. However, it was peculiarly suited to the spirit of chivalry, and grew rapidly in popu-

larity when feudalism gained a firm foothold, becoming at last the common form of trial for men of knightly rank.

This trial by combat, as it was sometimes called, was determined and judged by recognized rules. Forty days after a person was indicted, a piece of ground sixty feet square was marked off, and on one side was erected a place for the judges of the Court of Common Pleas, who attended in scarlet robes. A place was also provided for the lawyers. When the Court assembled, proclamations were made for accuser and accused, and they were brought into the inclosure by attendants or officers of the Court. Each officer was provided with a staff three feet, nine inches long, tipped with a horn, and each carried a four-cornered leather shield for defense. Graphic description of this kind of judicial combat was given by a nineteenth-century lawyer who said: [15]

". . . and the time being come, the heralds demanded silence; and the appellant was summoned three times by voice and by sound of trumpet. As he marched forward he was addressed by the Constable, 'Who are thou, and where-

177

fore comest thou armed to the door of these lists?' His answer given, he was taken to his pavilion, and afterwards was made to swear on the altar that his cause was just. The other did in like fashion. Then the pavilions were replaced by chairs whereon the combatants might take an occasional rest. Napkins holding a loaf and a bottle of water were hung on opposite ends of the lists. The marshal cried three times 'Laissez les aller,' and the pair went at it. Far better death than defeat. If either yielded, the marshal cried 'Hoo,' to declare the combat at an end. Then the wretch was taken to the scaffold on which his shield was hung reversed, his sword was broken, and his spurs hacked from his heels. He was now taken to the church where a mass for the dead was sung over him, and at last he was haled to the gibbet where the hangman claimed his prey."

It is interesting to note that this kind of trial started at sunrise and was not completed until the stars appeared, in which event the party charged was acquitted unless he had died in the meantime. If the accuser quit and pronounced the word "craven," the accused was set free.[16]

This peculiar method of legally fighting out one's legal disputes remained in effect in England as late as 1818.

"In England the end came in dramatic fashion. In May, 1817, Mary Ashford, a young woman of Langley in Warwickshire, was found drowned under suspicious circumstances. A certain Abram Thornton was suspected of the murder; he was tried and acquitted, but there was much evidence against him, and he had played so ill a part in a horrid though vulgar tragedy that the relatives of the dead girl cast about to carry the matter further. Now an old act pro-

178

vided that no acquittal by jury should bar an appeal of murder, so William Ashford, Mary's brother, appealed Thornton in the Court of King's Bench. He was attached, and when called upon pleaded 'Not guilty, and am ready to defend the same by my body.' He then threw down his glove on the floor of the Court. It was a curious turn; for no doubt men thought that he would put himself upon the country and stand a second trial by jury. There was much legal argument (November 17, 1817, to April 16, 1818), the prosecuting counsel tried hard to 'oust his battle,' (that is to prove this mode of trial by combat to be improper) but to no purpose, and in the end Thornton was set free. In 1819, two years after the drowning of Mary Ashford, the Appeal of Murder Act (59 Geo. III C. 46) abolished the last remnant of Wager of Battle."[17]

There was a time when women actually fought their own legal battles by personal combat. In Germany during the twelfth and thirteenth centuries, records show that the fairer

179

sex were permitted to "wage their own law." In the words of the famous historian, Henry Charles Lea:[18]

"The German laws refer to cases in which a woman might demand justice of a man personally in the lists, and not only are instances on record in which this was done, as in a case at Berne in 1128, in which the woman was the victor, but it was of sufficiently frequent occurrence to have an established mode of procedure which is preserved to us in all details by illuminated MSS. of the period. The chances between such unequal adversaries were adjusted by placing the man up to the navel in a pit three feet wide, tying his left hand behind his back, and arming him only with a club, while his fair opponent had the free use of her limbs and was furnished with a stone as large as the fist, or weighing from one to five pounds, fastened in a piece of stuff. A curious regulation provided the man with three clubs. If in delivering a blow he touched the earth with hand or arm he forfeited one of the clubs; if this happened thrice his last weapon was gone, he was adjudged defeated, and the woman could order his execution. On the other hand, the woman was similarly furnished with three weapons. If she struck the man while he was disarmed she forfeited one, and with the loss of the third she was at his mercy and was liable to be buried alive."

In civil cases the parties hired substitutes. This was especially true of women, priests, children, old men and cripples who appeared by champion, as they were naturally unable to fight in person. Finally this became a racket, and the "judicial combats" merely fights between hired gangs.

In criminal cases, the only participants in the affray were the actual parties themselves. The accused had the right not only to fight his accuser, but also to challenge a hostile witness and sometimes even a judge whom he charged with an unfair decision.

SOURCES

Chapter 10

1. Superstition and Force, by Henry Charles Lea (1892), pp. 359-370.
2. The Law's Lumber Room, by Francis Watt, p. 106.
3. Feudal System, by Cuming Walters, p. 70.
4. Credulities, Past and Present, Chatto and Windus, p. 33.
5. Ancient Laws, by Sir Henry Sumner Maine, p. 2107.
6. Trials in Medieval Boroughs of England, by Charles Gross, 15 H. L. R., 699.
7. The Law's Lumber Room, by Francis Watt, p. 98.
8. 15 Harvard Law Review, 700.
9. The Older Modes of Trial, by James B. Thayer, 5 H. L. R. (2), pp. 64, 65.
10. The Law's Lumber Room, by Francis Watt, pp. 102, 103.
11. Superstitions in Ancient Trials, by W. P. Rogers.
12. Readings of the History and Systems of the Common Law, by Pound and Pluncknett (3rd Ed.), 137.
13. The Law's Lumber Room, by Francis Watt, pp. 100, 101.
14. The Judicial Use of Torture, 11 H. L. R. (1), 220.
15. The Law's Lumber Room, by Francis Watt, pp. 115, 116.
16. Wager of Battle, by V. P. Lucas (Los Angeles Bar).
17. The Law's Lumber Room, by Francis Watt, pp. 118, 119.
18. Superstition and Force, by Henry Charles Lea.

CHAPTER 67.

REGULATING THE USE OF AUTOMOBILES.

An Act in relation to automobiles and motor vehicles, regulating their speed and operation on the public highways in this state, providing for their proper equipment, and providing penalties for the violation thereof.

Be it enacted by the Legislature of the State of Kansas:

SECTION 1. That the term "automobile" and "motor vehicle" as used in this act shall be construed to include all types and grades of motor vehicles propelled by electricity, steam, gasoline, or other source of energy, commonly known as automobiles, motor vehicles, or horseless carriages, using the public highways and not running on rails or tracks. Nothing in this section shall be construed as in any way preventing, obstructing, impeding, embarrassing or in any other manner or form infringing upon the prerogative of any political chaffeur to run an automobilious band-wagon at any rate he sees fit compatible with the safety of the occupants thereof; provided, however, that not less than ten nor more than twenty ropes be allowed at all times to trail behind this vehicle when in motion, in order to permit those who have been so fortunate as to escape with their political lives an opportunity to be dragged to death; and provided further, that whenever a mangled and bleeding political corpse implores for mercy, the driver of the vehicle shall, in accordance with the provisions of this bill, "Throw out the life-line."

CHAPTER 11

LUDICROUS LAWS

"Oh, sir, you understand a conscience, but not law."
—The Old Law, by Massinger

KANSAS AUTOMOBILE STATUTE

STUPID legislation has been identified with certain states at certain times. For example, at the turn of this century, Kansas enacted many stupid laws. One of the most glaring was the automobile statute reproduced in part on the opposite page.[1] According to former New York District Attorney Arthur Train, it was "passed presumably as a joke, on April 1, 1903." There is no question about its having been actually incorporated into the Revised Statutes of Kansas that year.

A CHANGE IN "PI"

Perhaps the "life-line law," as it was called, is no more absurd than the Kansas law which changed the meaning of the word "pi" from 3.1416 to an even three,[2] or the legal requirement that every able-bodied citizen between the ages of twenty-one and sixty should "kill grasshoppers one day each year."[3]

183

An earlier Kansas legislature is credited with having enacted the following freak law:

When two trains approach each other at a crossing, they shall both come to a full stop, and neither shall start up until the other has gone.[4]

LAND LIMITATIONS

Unusual land limitations have prevailed down to recent times. However, the law of the ancient Romans was most singular in this respect; it prohibited the ownership of more than thirty-two hundred square yards at any one time.[5]

A trace of the same general limitation was found existing during the time of Caesar among the German peoples.[6] The only difference was that the Germans could not legally hold the same land for more than one year.

JUDGES PENALIZED

The very ancient law punishing judges for changing their decisions should head the list of unsound laws. According to section 5, of Hammurabi's *Code:*

"If a judge pronounces a judgment, renders a decision, delivers a verdict duly signed and sealed and afterwards alters his judgment they shall call that judge to account for the alteration of the judgment which he had pronounced and he shall pay twelvefold the penalty which was in said judgment; and in the assembly they shall expel him from his seat of judgment, and he shall not return, and with the judges in a case he shall not take his seat."[7]

NO MANUAL LABOR

A famous Spartan leader by the name of Lycurgus drafted laws in the ninth century B. C. which remained in effect over a thousand years. One of his laws provided that a Spartan citizen could not perform any kind of manual labor during his lifetime. This has been explained on the theory that manual labor was regarded as beneath the dignity of a citizen, such being only the task of slaves.[8]

REQUIRED DRUNKENNESS

A Greek law made it a crime *not* to get drunk at the festival of Dionysia, sobriety being regarded as a symptom of ingratitude to the god of wine. Similarly, it was lawful among ancient Indians to kill a king, provided the killer was drunk.[9]

Perhaps one of the most fantastic laws ever promulgated in England was the one making it a crime to kill a fairy. During the reign of Henry III, "to wound, maym or kill a fairy" was punishable by death.

PROHIBITION OF BEARDS

Another set of foolish laws in force during medieval times related to prohibition of the wearing of beards.

In 1447, during the reign of King Henry VI, the Irish Parliament enacted a law, known as the Statute of Trim, which required all Irishmen to shave their upper lips; otherwise submit to immediate execution without trial by either court or jury. Incidentally, this senseless act obtained the name because it was inspired at Trim, Ireland.[10]

A similar statute was enacted in 1530 by virtue of a royal decree issued by Francis I of France. Three days after the decree was posted, it went into effect and banned the wearing of beards or whiskers. If the decree was disregarded, the beard-wearer paid the penalty of being hanged.[11]

ROQUEFORT CHEESE REQUIREMENTS

Another curious law was one decreed by King Charles VI. He approved the law that required real Roquefort cheese to be made from the milk of ewes, and not cows. This was announced so as to break up a monopoly by a group of Roquefort cheese manufacturers in Rouen, France who used cow's milk.[12]

Until 1834, it was lawful for any religious congregation in the city of New York to stretch chains across the street in front of its house of worship during the hours of service.[13]

LEAP YEAR ENFORCED

Scotland has had much ludicrous legislation. An example is the "leap-year" statute, which was enacted in 1228:

"It is statut and ordaint that during the rain of her maist blissit Majestie, for ilk yeare known as lepe year, ilk mayden ladye of bothe highe and lowe estate shall hae libertie to bespeke ye man she likes. Albeit he refuses to talk to her to be his lawful wyfe, he shall be mulcted in ye sum one pound or less, as his estait may be, except if he can make it appeare that he is betroth to any ither woman he then shall be free."[14]

CHRISTMAS PROHIBITED IN MASSACHUSETTS

Due to the unfounded allegations that Christmas was "anti-Christ Masse" says Washington Irving's *Sketch Book*, "The Flying Eagle," the General Court of Massachusetts passed a law in 1659 which provided:

"a fine of five shillings for every offense if a body be found observing by abstinence from work, by celebrating or attending a religious service . . . such a day as Christmas day."

The law was not repealed until 1681.[15]

CHRISTMAS PROHIBITED

The foolish law prohibiting the celebration of Christmas in Scotland is another typical illustration. Since 1644, this

187

Parliamentary Act has been in effect. The reason for the banning of all Christmas celebration was because it was regarded as a heathen festival.[16] It has never been repealed. In this connection, it is interesting to note that for eighteen years England forbade the celebration of Christmas.

THE BULL OF ADRIAN

In 1170, an Englishman could legally murder an Irishman without incurring any penalty.[17] This unusual license was proclaimed in the Bull of Adrian.

FOOD RESTRICTIONS

In 1336 the Ordinance of Edward III prohibited any Englishman from having more than two courses at any one meal. Each mess was limited to two sorts of victuals and, except on certain feast days, one could mix sauce with his pottage only in a certain way.[18]

FEMININE EMBELLISHMENTS FORBIDDEN

Women who compromised Englishmen by wearing bustles, paint and perfume were legally ostracized by the English Parliament in 1770, when it enacted:

"That all women, of whatever age, rank, profession, or degree, whether virgins, maids or widows, that shall, from and after such act, impose upon, seduce, and betray into matrimony any of his Majesty's subjects by the scents, paints, cosmetic washes, artificial teeth, false hair, Spanish wool, iron stays, hoops, high-heeled shoes, bolstered hips, shall incur the penalty of the law in force against witchcraft and like misdemeanors, and that the marriage upon conviction shall stand null and void."[19]

THE PRICE OF A WIFE IN VIRGINIA

The Virginia County Records, compiled by the Earl of Southhampton, disclose that in 1621, in Virginia, 120 pounds of tobacco was the legal rate of exchange for a wife.[20]

UNITED STATES LEGAL MEASURE

By virtue of Congressional act of 1893, the United States adopted the international meter (which equals 3.28 feet) as its legal standard. Contrary to general impression, neither the yard nor the foot is the official legal standard of measure.

MASSACHUSETTS BLUE LAWS

Some of the most foolish legislation ever found on the statute books had its origin in Massachusetts. In 1632, the following law was enacted in Massachusetts:

"No female garment shall be made with short sleeves— where the nakedness of the arm may be discovered thereof."[21]

Violators of this decree were severely punished.

A year later, it was ordered:

"that no person, householder or other shall spend his time idly or unprofitably under pain of such punishment as the county court shall think best to inflict."[22]

In 1741, Massachusetts legislated against the giving of scarfs, gloves, wine, rum and rings at funerals, because they were regarded as unnecessary expenses.[23]

The first speed law in the United States was a Boston ordinance, enacted in 1757. It read:

"Coaches, sleighs, chairs and other carriages shall not be driven through the streets faster than a walking pace—or interfere with the Sabbath worship.

"A fine of ten shillings will be exacted from the master of the slave or servant so driving."[24]

DISTRIBUTION OF LAWYERS

The legislature of New York passed an act on October 22, 1695, which prohibited the hiring of more than two lawyers for any case. The Colonial law provided:

"Whereas the number of Attorneys-at-Law that practice at the Barr in this Province are but few and that many persons Retain most of them on one side to the great prejudice and discouragement of others that have or may have suits at Law to the end therefore that Justice may be Equally administered and no Room Left for Complaint be it Enacted by the Governor and Council and Representatives Convened in Generall Assembly and by the Authority of the same that from and after the publication hereof that no person or persons That shall have any suit at Law in any of the Courts of Record Within this Province shall Retain more than two Attorneys at Law for the prosecution or management of any such Suit or process at Law that they shall have and if they Retain any more it shall be Lawful for the Justices of the bench where the Suit is Depending to order all such Attorneys as shall be Retained more than two, as aforesaid to plead for the other side Without Returning the fee Received any thing Contained in this or any other Act to the Contrary hereof in any wise Notwithstanding, provided That this Act

Nor any thing Contained therein shall Continue in force any Longer than two years after the publiction hereof."[25]

NO WOMEN SMOKERS IN NEW YORK

The City Council of New York passed an ordinance in 1908 which made it illegal for women to smoke in any public place in New York City.[26] New York newspapers had carried headlines that "women were seen smoking on their way to the opera." A San Francisco dispatch said that a "New York woman of some social importance has been brave enough to give the European custom of women smoking the seal of American approval." The result of all this publicity was to cause the enactment of the Sullivan Ordinance, on January 21, 1908, which specifically banned women from smoking publicly anywhere in the city. The ordinance, needless to say, has since been repealed.

MARY WALKER'S TROUSERS

Even Congress has passed foolish laws. Among them was the special Congressional Act which permitted Dr. Mary Walker to wear trousers the rest of her life.[27]

When the Civil War began Mary Edwards Walker, then twenty-nine years of age, joined up with the medical corps and thereafter completely discarded female attire. Because of her bravery, she was decorated with the Congressional Medal and commissioned a first lieutenant in the United States army. The well-known physician and suffragette died in 1919, having attained the unusual distinction of legally dressing in male attire for over fifty years.

191

THE CONGRESSIONAL RECORD HONORS A GEORGIAN

Another entertaining bit of Congressional action is found in Volume 78, page 6 of the *Congressional Record* for April 17, 1934.[28]

Congressman Blanton of Georgia announced the death of a constituent. Remarks of a short newspaper account were read into the *Congressional Record*, as follows:

"Savannah, Georgia, April 15, 1934—Mrs. Belle Rhynes, one-hundred-and-twenty-three-year-old Irishwoman, who attributed her long life to pipe smoking and a philosophic outlook, died today at the Little Sisters of the Poor Home. She was born in Dublin, March 4, 1811, and came to America with her parents, Mr. and Mrs. Thomas Heights, when eleven years old. In early life she joined a circus with her husband, now many years dead, and performed as a snake charmer . . .

WHO
SAYS LAWYERS
AREN'T SUCKERS?

"Last year Mrs. Rhynes took a marked interest in the political situation when Franklin D. Roosevelt was inaugurated President on her birthday. She had just recovered from an illness when she learned of the inauguration, and breakfasted in bed, topping things off by smoking her pipe; she never tried cigarettes. She said she had asthma for a hundred and one years, but had been cured of that."

WHEN IS A LAWYER A FISH?

The act shown in the illustration was passed in 1907. Many members of the legal profession rose up in arms, citing it as another one of those crazy laws. However, the word "lawyer," as used in the above sense, refers to a certain species of fish that inhabits Michigan waters.[29]

NO ENGLISH AUTHORITIES

For years there was a law on the statute books of Kentucky which forbade the citation of English authorities in courts of law.[30]

UNCONSCIOUS LAWLESSNESS

A former city attorney[31] of Ludlow, Kentucky, made the following comments upon the laws of his own home town:

"When a man opens his door to admit a stray dog he is harboring an unlicensed animal; fine $100. He extracts a cigaret from a package without destroying the stamp; fine $50 and six months in jail. He reads a detective story magazine and becomes a law breaker for having in his possession a book principally made up of 'accounts of criminal deeds'; ten days, a fine of $1000 or ten days to a year in jail. He bets a 5-cent cigar; $100 fine. He backs an automobile across a pavement, $5 fine. It backfires, $10 fine. He forgets to put on his auto license plates, fine $10 to $100. He fails to exhibit city license tags, fine $10 to $100. He runs through a 'stop' signal, fine $5. He fails to signal while turning a corner; fine $10 to $100. He swerves to the left of the center of the streetcar; fine $10 to $100. Thus the ordinary man in the course of an ordinary day's events becomes liable to fines totaling $3,939, court costs amounting to $310 and imprisonment for 725 days. All this becomes possible under 30,000 statutes and ordinances of which common law presumes everyone to have knowledge."

FOOD IN ENGLISH

In Wisconsin, there was a statute which required all bills of fare to be printed in English. This law was not quite as bad, however, as the Montana food law which still provides: [32]

"Sec. 8513. If a proprietor, manager or other person having the management of any hotel, restaurant or boarding house in the State of Montana shall serve or cause to be served upon the tables to his or their guests an article of food known to said proprietor or manager of said hotel, restaurant or boarding house, to be adulterated, he shall be guilty of violation of this Act, unless he or they shall have posted, hung up and maintained in his or their dining room, in a conspicuous place in full view of his or their guests, a large red, cardboard sign, the size of which shall be twelve (12) inches in width, the words printed thereon in large bold black letters of the size of not less than seventy-two-point type—

'WE SERVE ON OUR TABLES NO FOOD STUFFS WHICH HAVE BEEN HARMFULLY ADULTERATED.' "

195

An often-violated law of the United States is the one which makes it a crime for anyone to write a check for less than one dollar.[33] Difficult as it is to believe, this act still remains on the Federal Statute books. It provides:

"No person shall make, issue, circulate or pay out any note, check, memorandum, token or other obligation for less than one dollar intended to circulate as money in the United States; and every person so offending shall be fined not more than $500 or imprisoned not more than six months or both." (Sec. 178, F. S. P. L.)

Perhaps the most stupid statute of them all is the Illinois act which makes it illegal to speak English anywhere in the State of Illinois.[34] Ever since 1923 this has stood on the statute books of that state. The legislation was adopted after "Big Bill" Thompson, former Chicago mayor, so vehemently voiced an anti-English attitude. It declares:

"The official language of the State of Illinois shall be known hereafter as the American language."

CHIEF JUSTICE DIXON'S IRONY

In closing this chapter it might be well to note the following choice morsel of irony rendered by Chief Justice Dixon, in 1871, in the case of *Owens v. State*, 27 Wis. 456 at 458:

"In thus considering the act, we cannot forbear remarking it as a most singular instance of the sparing hand of legislation in this state, that there should still be found upon our books a statute so old as this, the work of the first legislative body assembled after our organization and admission as a state. It stands, we believe, without rival or peer, as the only statute of the state of Wisconsin which has been permitted to attain the venerable age of nearly twenty-three years. This leads to the serious reflections as to the untimely fate of most of our legislative enactments not only the companions of this, which have long since 'faded and gone,' but also those which have come after, a numerous progeny, nearly all of which seem to have been infected with some fatal disease, which was very soon to work their destruction. They have perished mostly in infancy, the average period of life being about one year; but those which have survived that period have seldom attained the age of ten or twelve. There must be something irregular and wrong in the birth and parentage, where such mortality prevails among the offspring—some malady and restlessness in the body politic, which demand the most careful attention and cure. The act under consideration is certainly entitled to our utmost veneration and respect by reason of that health and vigor that have enabled it to outlive so many thousands of its brethren, which have fainted and fallen by the way."

SOURCES

Chapter 11

1. Laws of Kansas (1903), Chapter 67, Sec. 413.
2. Our Fool Legislatures.
3. Ohio Bar Association Report, Vol. IX, No. 26, p. 351.
4. On the Trail of Bad Men, by Arthur Train.
5. Page on Wills, Vol. 1, Par. 5, p. 9.
6. Caesar's Commentaries, Book IV, Chap. 22.

7. Code of Hammurabi, Sec. 5.

8. Lycurgus' Permanent Laws.

9. Curiosities of Law and Lawyers, by Croake James, pp. 438, 439.

10. Statute of Trim (1442).

11. Receuils des Ordinances, Folio 48, Paris, 1557.

12. Illinois Law Review (1934-35).

13. Harper's Weekly, March 13, 1880, p. 163, col. 3.

14. Ohio Law Reporter, pp. 183, 184.

15. Enzyklopadie für Theologie und Kirche, by Weihnachten.

16. Laws of Scotland (1644).

17. Studies in Church History, by Holloway Henry, p. 52.

18. Curiosities of Law and Lawyers, by Croake James, p. 79.

19. 52 Law Notes (England), p. 355.

20. The Virginia County Records, by Earl of Southampton.

21. Laws of Massachusetts (1632).

22. The Legal Blues, by William F. Craig, p. 91.

23. The Legal Blues, by William F. Craig, p. 91.

24. Ordinance enacted 1757, Boston, Mass.

25. Colonial Laws of New York, Vol. 1, Chap. 49.

26. Our Times (Pre-War American), by Mark Sullivan, p. 532.

27. Our Times (1900-1925), by Mark Sullivan, p. 411.

28. Congressional Record, Vol. 78, part 6.

29. Public Acts (Michigan, 1907), No. 239, p. 307.

30. Our Foolish Legislatures.

31. Richard Carran.

32. Revised Code of Montana of 1907. 10th Session, Chapter 169, Sec. 8513.

33. U. S. Code Annotated, Title 18, Par. 293 (1909).

34. Smith-Hurd Illinois Revised Statutes (1935), Chap. 127, Par. 177, pp. 3100, 3101.

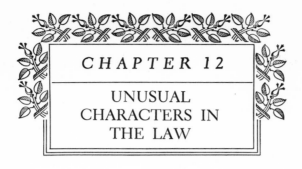

CHAPTER 12

UNUSUAL
CHARACTERS IN
THE LAW

"The first thing we do;
Let's kill all the lawyers."
—*King Henry VI*, William Shakespeare

THROUGHOUT the memory of man, stories have been handed down concerning outstanding legal characters. Much has been legend, but a great deal has been based upon fact.

Let us turn back several centuries to begin a complete roll of persons who belong to the class of curious characters in the law. Certain members of the Bar have been outstanding for performing heroic deeds and enduring tremendous physical hardships just to gain a point for a client (who may or may not have appreciated it). It is the purpose of the next few pages to bring to light a few notable illustrations of such admirable lawyers as well as others who are merely eccentric.

DEMOSTHENES

Demosthenes, the greatest trial lawyer that ever lived, was afflicted with hesitation of speech during boyhood and early manhood.[1] Despite this handicap, he took to trial work and

199

subsequently defended Ctesiphon before a jury consisting of a thousand people. His greatest speech was the "restoration on the crown" which became the masterpiece of the ancient Greek world.

SAINT IVES

Another outstanding character in the annals of legal fame is Saint Ives.[2] He was one of the few lawyers ever made a saint. In the churchyard of St. Mimihy, at Trequier, Brittany, is the tomb where rest the remains of Yves Heloury de Kermartin, allegedly the only lawyer who ever became ordained. It was in the thirteenth century that he was chosen a saint for the University of Sapienza, in Rome. Most people said of him:

"He was a lawyer, yet not a rascal, and the people were astonished."

EGOTISM

The most conceited lawyer that ever lived was Charles Dumoulin.[3] Although he was recognized by historians as

a leading member of the bar during the sixteenth century, his egotism is without parallel. He began each one of his legal opinions with the Latin phrase: *Ego a nemine doceri possum,* meaning, "Nobody can teach me the law."

STEPHEN JOHNSON FIELD

Among these celebrated personalities in the law was the late Stephen Johnson Field.[4] His thirty-four years on the United States Supreme Court bench gave him the distinction of having served that court longer than anyone else; and though his many opinions have rightfully been regarded as great contributions to the law, his name will be better remembered because of the part he played in the facts surrounding the famous Federal case known as *"In re Neagle."*

Born in Haddam, Connecticut, in 1816, Justice Field was educated in the East, but, when thirty-three, migrated to California during the time of the gold rush in '49. A flirtatious beauty by the name of Sarah Althea Hill also moved out to San Francisco at that time and subsequently became the mistress of rich old United States Senator William Sharon, who was known as "King of the Comstock Lode." After fifteen months, the Senator had her thrown out of his hotel. Finally the siren succeeded in wangling out "a fat cash settlement," according to *Time* Magazine, but several years later sued the Senator in State Court for breach of promise, producing letters and papers which, if genuine, indicated they were man and wife. Suit was brought in Federal Court by the Senator, who declared the papers were forgeries. A divorce suit followed wherein the sensational beauty charged Sharon with

adultery and desertion. Her lawyer was David Smith Terry,
a big, raw-boned Texan who had been Chief Justice of the
California Supreme Court. A widower, he soon fell in love
with his client and married her.

In the meantime, Justice Field, who had succeeded Terry,
his long-time political foe, as Chief Justice of the State Court,
was appointed in 1863 by President Lincoln as an Associate
Justice of the United States Supreme Court. Not long after,
Senator Sharon died and his heirs brought suit in the Federal
Circuit Court to cancel the claims of Mrs. Sarah Althea
Terry. Justice Field was then on regular circuit duty and as
he was announcing a decision against the hot-tempered Sarah
Althea, she asked how much the Sharon people had paid him
for the opinion. The judge instructed U. S. Deputy Mar-
shal David Neagle to remove Mrs. Terry from the court-
room. Before the marshal could get hold of the irate woman,
her outraged husband sent him sprawling across the room.
Both of the Terrys were finally caught, and after being disarmed were jailed for being in contempt of court. "When
I get out of jail," Terry allegedly said, "I'll horsewhip Judge
Field, and if he resents it, I'll kill him."

He had his chance in the summer of 1889. Justice Field and his bodyguard, U. S. Deputy Marshal David Neagle, had been eating in the railroad station lunchroom at Lathrop, California. Just as they were about ready to leave, in walked the Terrys. As soon as Mrs. Terry noticed the Judge, she turned on her heel and disappeared. Her husband walked right up behind Field, however, and slapped the Associate Justice on the back. Just then Neagle shot Terry dead. For this both Justice Field and his Deputy Marshal were arrested for murder. The case against the Judge was soon dropped after the Governor had intervened. The case against Neagle, however, was carried to the United States Supreme Court, which ruled in favor of the Deputy Marshal, announcing the proposition that Federal officers while in the course of their duty are not within the reach of state courts.[5]

Justice Field lived to eighty-three. Sarah Althea Terry outlived him by more than thirty years, not dying until 1937 (although she had been an inmate of an insane asylum in Stockton, California, ever since her husband, Terry, was shot) .

A COURT FILIBUSTER

Louis Bernard was one of the most unusual lawyers in all France. He saved a client's life in 1816 by speaking incessantly for five days in order to obtain a delay. General Jean Travot was on trial before a special courtmartial in Rennes and Bernard was his chief legal defender. The general had been charged with treason and the military court condemned him to death. In order to stay the death sentence, "a delay of several days was solicited by the defenders of the accused." Bernard, the lawyer, arbitrarily delayed the sentence by making such a long speech requesting the delay.

The sentence was appealed but the reviewing court confirmed it. However, King Louis XVIII commuted the death sentence to twenty years confinement in prison, and two years later released the unfortunate general who had then become insane. Monsieur Bernard's appeal was regarded by some magistrates as an abuse of the rights of the defense.[6]

JUDGMENTS FROM HIS BED

Judge M. Halloin, of Cam, France, never had a sick day in his life; yet he pronounced all his judgments from his bed.

He was a great lover of tranquillity and ease, and so he exercised his functions as Justice of the Peace from his bedside, pronouncing sentence with his head resting on a pillow and his body languidly extended on the feather bed.

Even his will carried out his ever-restful thought; for it provided a clause which expressed his wish to be buried in his bed, comfortably tucked in with pillows and coverlets, as he had died. As no objection was raised against the execution of the clause, a huge pit was sunk and the decedent was lowered into his final resting-place without any alteration having been made in the position in which death had overtaken him.[7]

ANIMAL DEFENDER

Another curious character found in the legal ranks is the French lawyer, Bartholomew de Chassenée. As noted in Chapter II, he gained legal favor in the sixteenth century for having defended rats charged with stealing a barley crop in Burgundy. Born in 1480 in Issy-l'Ereque, the adroit counsellor won his first laurels in the celebrated *"cause des rats"* in 1510. Later he became known as a professional defender of animals charged with crime, and enjoyed a high reputation at the French Bar.[8]

One of the most illustrious legal personages was William Blackstone. Yet between 1746 and 1760, he was supposedly a failure as a lawyer, because he engaged in only two cases. However, that period was devoted to legal writing, and on June 23, 1753, at Oxford, he delivered the first lecture ever given on English common law. His compiled lectures, *Blackstone's Commentaries*, gained him lasting fame.[9]

PERSISTENCE

Lord Erskine tried a case before a jury that sat for twenty-one consecutive hours.[10] On August 27, 1788, a notorious character, William (Deacon) Brodie, went on trial for robbery before a jury in Edinburgh, Scotland. Lord Braxfield presided. Due to the belief that a felony trial should not be adjourned, the jury sat for twenty-one hours straight before it retired to deliberate. Brodie was found guilty, and on October 1st of that same year he was hanged.

TWENTY THOUSAND DEATH SENTENCES

There have been many dual personalities engaged in the practice of law. A leading example was Judge Carpzov of the Leipzig Court of Appeals, who pronounced over twenty thousand death sentences and yet read through the entire Bible fifty-three times.[11]

HIGHWAYMAN JUDGE

Another judge who possessed a dual makeup was Sir John Popham of England. He was a most peculiar character at the Bar. In 1519, he became Lord Chief Justice. Because of his merciless sentences, especially toward highway robbers, he became known as the "hanging judge." History reveals, however, that while Sir John was preparing for the Bar, he fell in with bad company and eventually headed a band of highway robbers until he got married, whereupon he reformed. His relentlessness toward criminals later became a byword among notorious highwaymen. Incidentally, Sir John Popham was the judge who sentenced Sir Walter Raleigh to death.[12]

DISRAELI

Still another curious character in the eyes of the law was Disraeli. For on November 22, 1838, the one-time Prime Minister of England was indicted, charged with criminal libel, for having made the statement that the legal profession appeared to be exempt from libel, judging the license given a certain barrister by the name of Austin whose article infuriated Disraeli, then a candidate for Parliament. Although the Prime Minister defaulted by way of answer, the Queen's Bench dismissed the indictment upon Austin's request due to Disraeli's public letter of apology to the Bench and Bar.[13] So even one of the world's greatest diplomats has tangled and untangled with the law.

THE WORLD'S LARGEST POLITICAL MEETING

The famous Irish lawyer, Daniel O'Connell, was responsible for the world's largest political meeting. It was on August

15, 1843, that this great political orator spoke from the ancient hill of Tara, Ireland, to over a million persons who came from all parts of the world in an effort to save Ireland's independence and repeal legislation making the Emerald Isle a part of England.[14]

THE LONGEST QUESTION

Robert M. Morse, of the Boston Bar, propounded the longest hypothetical question ever asked in a courtroom. It contained twenty thousand words. The question, which took the interrogator over three hours to propound, concerned the mental condition of a testator and was put to Dr. Jelley, a Boston expert on insanity, in the famous Tuckerman will contest in Suffolk Probate Court. Judge McKim, who presided over the trial, reported that Mr. Morse began his question with the opening of court and did not complete it until noon adjournment. Incidentally, the answer comprised just three words, "I don't know."[15]

ANOTHER LONG ONE

During the Harry K. Thaw trial, District Attorney Jerome submitted a hypothetical question, which consisted of approximately fifteen thousand words, the reading of which occupied nearly an entire session of court. The same question (it dealt with insanity) was put to six different experts. One of these was a Dr. Smith Ely Jelliffe, who thirty years later sued Thaw for his unpaid fee, which he placed at $10,250. A Federal jury awarded the alienist only $750.

LAWYERS' FEES

Most people have exaggerated notions about lawyers' fees. For instance, Dudley Field was awarded three-tenths of a cent for six years' legal services rendered in the celebrated New York case of *Wright* v. *Boos*.[16] On the other hand, John G. Johnson of Philadelphia left a five-million-dollar estate, made almost entirely from the law. He obtained $100,-000 for his services in one case alone. Mr. Johnson undoubtedly earned more by way of legal fees than any other American lawyer. Scores of corporations paid him substantial yearly retainers just in case he might be needed.

LAW-PHOBIA

Perhaps the most peculiar American lawyer of the nineties was Charles F. Southmayde. He was so fearful that he might become a lawbreaker that he employed counsel to watch the many statutes introduced in the New York Legislature lest he might commit some crime that would subject him to incarceration.[17]

RATS !

Reference is made in Volume 2, page 280, of the *Ohio Law Reporter*, to what is "probably the shortest address ever given to a jury in the United States." It was made in 1904 "by Prosecuting Attorney Hooper in Justice Merritt's court in Battle Creek, Michigan. Dell Davis, a well-known character about town, was charged with the larceny of a whip from a farmer's buggy. Davis' attorney made a long speech to the jury, claiming that Davis only borrowed the whip to kill a rat. When he got through, Prosecutor Hooker arose, looked at the jury and exclaimed 'RATS' and sat down. The jury convicted Davis at once."

A COURAGEOUS JUDGE

One of the most perseverant men at the Bar is David Moylan, who has been a judge of the Municipal Court of Cleveland since 1915. Though he has no arms, Judge Moylan writes out his own charges to the jury, and signs all of his own court records by holding a pen between his teeth.

In 1898, he lost his right arm while working as a railway switchman.[18] Seven years later another accident deprived him of his left arm. However, he was determined to succeed. Judge Moylan practiced penmanship and eventually learned how to write quite legibly with an ordinary pen held between his teeth. Subsequently he studied law, passing the Ohio Bar. Several years of practice then followed. In 1912, he was elected to the City Council of Cleveland, and three years later he ran for the municipal bench and was successful.

Besides this unusual feat of being able to write, though armless, Judge Moylan can answer his own telephone and put on his own hat.

There was a time when the Judge refused to wear an overcoat even though the temperature was zero outside. His explanation was that to bundle up was conducive to colds and to go without an overcoat built up his resistance.

In former years, the author had the good fortune to try many cases before this court and often marveled at the way Judge Moylan personally "turned" the pages of his book while charging the jury. He did it with his tongue. If you think this is easy, just try it sometime.

SOURCES

Chapter 12

1. Panorama of the World's Legal Systems, by John H. Wigmore, Vol. 1, pp. 326, 335.

2. St. Yves; Patron of Lawyers, by Hugh Allen.

3. Panorama of the World's Legal Systems, by John H. Wigmore, Vol. 31, p. 1022.

4. Stephen J. Field, Craftsman of the Law, by Carl Brent Swisher.

5. In re Neagle, 135 U. S. 1, 10 Sup. Ct. Rep. 685, Time, the Weekly Newsmagazine, March 1, 1937, p. 15.

6. Biographies Nouvelles des Contemporains, Vol. XX, pp. 56-59, Paris, 1825.

Grande Dictionnaire Universelle, by Larousse, Vol. II, p. 597, and
Vol. XV, p. 448.
Biographie Universelle, by Michaud, Vol. 42, p. 101.

7. Curiosities of Olden Times, by S. Baring-Gould, pp. 50, 51.

8. Credulities, Past and Present, by William Jones, pp. 298, 299.

9. Blackstone as a Lawyer, by David A. Lockmiller.

10. Famous Trials of History, by Rt. Hon. Earl Birkenhead, p. 183.

11. Panorama of the World's Legal Systems, by John H. Wigmore,
Vol. 31, p. 1018.

12. Records of Wellington, Somersetshire, England.

13. Romantic Trials of Three Centuries, by Hugh Childers, p. 267.

14. The London Times, August 15, 1843.

15. 5 Ohio Law Reporter 45.

16. Celebrated Trials, by Henry L. Clinton, p. 342.

17. On the Trail of Bad Men, by Arthur Train, p. 153.

18. The Outlook, January 5, 1916, Vol. 112, p. 30.

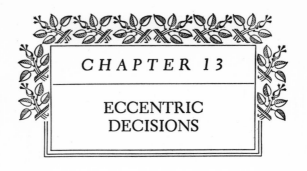

CHAPTER 13

ECCENTRIC DECISIONS

"Drink and forget the law."
—Proverbs 31:5

REALLY absurd legal decisions are not often found in law books. However, I have run across a few and they are worth citing.

METHUSELAH OF THE LAW

An English court refused to indulge in the presumption that a 792-year-old man was dead. It held that it could not judicially presume that a person alive in 1034 was not still living in 1826.[1]

A DISTURBING SINGER

A North Carolina trial judge found that one William Linkhaw was guilty of disturbing religious worship by singing church hymns out of tune. Fortunately, the State Supreme Court set aside the lower court's decision, saying:[2]

"The evidence as detailed by several witnesses was substantially this: Defendant is a member of the Methodist

214

Church; he sings in such a way as to disturb the congregation; at the end of each verse, his voice is heard after all the other singers have ceased. One of the witnesses being asked to describe defendant's singing, imitated it by singing a verse in the manner and voice of the defendant, which 'produced a burst of prolonged and irresistible laughter, convulsing alike the spectators, the bar, the jury and the court.'

"It was in evidence that the disturbance occasioned by the defendant's singing was decided and serious; the effect of it was to make one part of the congregation laugh, and the other mad; that the irreligious and frivolous enjoyed it as fun, while the serious and devout were indignant. It was also in evidence (without objection) that the congregation had been so much disturbed by it that the preacher had declined to sing the hymn, and shut up the book without singing it; that the presiding elder had refused to preach in the church on account of the disturbance occasioned by it; and that on one occasion a leading member of the church, appreciating that there was a feeling of solemnity prevading the congregation in consequence of the sermon just delivered, and fearing that it would be turned into ridicule, went to the defendant and asked him not to sing, and that on that occasion he did not sing. It also appeared that on many occasions the church members and authorities expostulated with the defendant about his singing and the disturbance growing out of it. To all of which he replied:

"That he would worship his God and that as part of his worship it was his duty to sing."

UNITED STATES V. 350 CARTONS OF CANNED SARDINES

The alleged violation of a Federal law relating to shipment and branding of canned sardines was presented to a jury, in

216

the case of *United States* v. *350 Cartons of Canned Sardines,* which returned the following verdict: [3]

"The jury finds a verdict in favor of the United States and recommends the mercy of the Court."

Judge Gibson, then presiding, smiled and said:

"We will take your recommendation of mercy under consideration."

LAWYERS CAN CRY

A lawyer has a right to shed tears before a jury. That is what the Supreme Court of Tennessee said in *Ferguson* v. *Moore,* 98 Tenn. 342. The pertinent part of the decision reads as follows:

"The conduct of counsel in presenting their cases to juries is a matter which must be left largely to the ethics of the profession and the discretion of the trial judge. Perhaps no two counsel observe the same rules in presenting their cases to the jury. Some deal wholly in logic and argument, without embellishments of any kind; others use rhetoric and occasional flights of fancy and imagination; others employ only noise and gesticulation, relying upon their earnestness and vehemence, instead of logic and rhetoric; others appeal to the

217

sympathies—it may be the passions and peculiarities—of the jurors; others combine all these, with variations and accompaniments of different kinds. Tears have always been considered legitimate arguments before a jury. . . . It would appear to be one of the natural rights of counsel which no court or constitution could take away. It is certainly, if no more, a matter of the highest personal privilege. Indeed, if counsel has them at command, it may be seriously questioned whether it is not his professional duty to shed them whenever proper occasion arises, and the trial judge would not feel constrained to interfere unless they were indulged in to such extent as to impede or delay the business of the court."

JUDGES' GEMS

Judges usually avoid the ridiculous. However, some of them have indulged in loose language, as evidenced by the following excerpts taken from reported legal opinions:

"For some time *after* his death, plaintiff in error, John G. Holmes, worked in a brewery as an employee of Mrs. Walter, who had charge of the business for herself and children." *Holmes* v. *State*, 102 N.W. 321.

". . . From which mortal wound he, the said Hurva Garnett, then and there died, contrary to the form of the statute." . . . *Potter* v. *State*, 162 Ind. 213 at 214.

". . . One would not think of going to a butcher shop to obtain a musical instrument, except under the fallacy of making a whistle of a pig's tail." *Grinnell* v. *Asiuliewicz*, 241 Mich. 190.

"Oysters are wild animals." *State* v. *Johnson*, 141 Pac. 1040 (Washington).

"Effie is an old jade of fifty summers, Jessie a frisky filly of forty, and Addie, the flower of the family, a capering monstrosity of thirty-five. Effie is spavined, Addie is stringhalt, and Jessie, the only one who showed her stockings, has legs with calves as classic in their outlines as the curves of a broom handle." *Cherry v. Des Moines Leader,* 114 Iowa 298.

The above statement was decided not to be libelous in the State of Iowa.

DAMAGES FOR BARKING DOGS

In Ohio the owner of a dog which barks an automobilist off the road may be liable for damages, according to *Von Rohr v. Silverglade,* 22 Ohio Nisi Prius (n.s.) 333.

SHAKESPEARE NOT THE AUTHOR

Judge Richard S. Tuthill of Chicago ruled in 1916 that William Shakespeare had nothing to do with the writing of the Shakespearean plays. At last, thought the legal profession, this great question has been finally settled! However, before the year was out, the Court changed his mind and withdrew his entry. So the burning question still remains unsolved.[4]

In August of 1939, there appeared in a well-known law journal the following legal opinion of a *lawsuit which never existed*.

S. Bartikean v. X. Bardos.
Municipal Court of Cleveland.
(Decided July 25, 1939.)

Husband and wife—Alienation of affections—Acts on part of parent not actionable, when—Limitations where acts committed in another state—Accord and satisfaction—Rescission.

1. [PAGE] *Husband and Wife* § 107.
When a parent is prompted by a sincere desire to promote the welfare and happiness of his child, and advises such child in good faith to leave her husband, such acts on the part of the parent are not actionable unless his conduct is malicious.

2. [PAGE] *Husband and Wife* § 109.
Where, in an action for alienation of affections brought in an Ohio court, the acts complained of were committed by the defendant while he was in the state of New York, the law of that forum will prevail.

3. [PAGE] *Accord and Satisfaction* § 10.
Where persons have voluntarily settled their differences by an accord and satisfaction, the courts will not reopen the controversy without a showing of fraud, mistake or duress.

[PAGE] For other cases, see same topic and number in Page's *Ohio Digest*, Lifetime Edition.

W. H. Stone, of Cleveland, for plaintiff.

J. H. Read, of Cleveland, for defendant.

COPLAND, J.

On and prior to October 10, 1936, the plaintiff and his wife, who was the daughter of the defendant, resided in Cleveland, while the defendant was a resident of Buffalo, N. Y. On said date the wife of the plaintiff instituted divorce proceedings in Cleveland against the plaintiff and shortly thereafter, because of plaintiff's alleged aggressions, she left him and took up her residence temporarily with her parents in Buffalo. It seems some years ago the defendant operated two businesses of similar character, one in Buffalo and the other in Cleveland. It is admitted that the entire capital contribution of said enterprises was made by the defendant.

It seems further that in 1931 the entire management of the Cleveland store was turned over to the plaintiff (the son-in-law of the defendant) by the defendant, and all of the profits of said store were drawn by and paid to the plaintiff until December 5, 1936, when defendant came to Cleveland, took physical possession of said store and discharged plaintiff, after which date plaintiff received no further remuneration from the operation of said store. Some few months later, defendant with his family including his daughter, Mrs. Bartikean, established his domicile in Cleveland.

In April, 1937, plaintiff instituted suit against the defendant, claiming he was a partner in the Cleveland store with the defendant and praying for a dissolution of said partnership and an accounting.

It seems further that for the purpose of amicably composing the litigation between the plaintiff and his wife and the plaintiff and the defendant, an agreement was drawn up in

221

the office of plaintiff's counsel on September 14, 1937, by the terms of which plaintiff's wife waived all alimony for herself; that plaintiff was to pay a stipulated amount monthly for the support of his two children; that he in turn was to be given the privilege of seeing his children on certain definite occasions; and as to the controversy between the plaintiff and defendant, it was agreed between them (in writing) that in consideration of the sum of $3,000 paid by defendant to plaintiff, each of the parties released the other from any and all claims of any nature, kind and description which either had or may have against the other from the beginning of time to the date thereof. The money was duly paid by the defendant to the plaintiff and the case of plaintiff against defendant marked "Settled and dismissed at plaintiff's costs," and subsequently the divorce matter was duly heard in court and a decree granted the wife of plaintiff, in which decree was incorporated the agreement of the parties with respect to alimony and custody of the children.

On January 15, 1938, after these various litiguous matters between the various parties hereinbefore referred to were disposed of, plaintiff instituted the instant suit against the defendant for alienation of affections. This matter duly came on for trial and at the conclusion thereof, on motion by defendant, finding was made in favor of defendant and plaintiff's petition was dismissed at his costs. This matter now comes before this court on a motion for a new trial duly made by plaintiff.

This case could have been disposed of on any one of three grounds which this court will go into.

In cases of alienation of affections, the motive with which the defendant acted is an element controlling on the question of his liability, and it must appear that he acted from improper motives. However, it is fundamental that when a parent—or one standing *in loco parentis*—is prompted by a sincere desire to promote the welfare and happiness of his child, and advises such child in good faith to leave her husband, such acts on the part of the parent are not actionable unless his conduct is malicious. *Westlake v. Westlake*, 34 Ohio St., 621; *Bourne v. Bourne*, 43 Cal. A. 516; *Bennett v. Smith*, 21 Barb. 439.

As was stated by the learned court in *Lanigan v. Lanigan*, 222 Mass., 198:

"If a father from hostility and ill will to his son's wife, brings about a separation, such wife has a cause of action for damages. On the other hand, a father is under no liability for honest advice to separate, given his son, from parental affection."

And in the instant case there is no credible testimony other than that the defendant advised his daughter what to do and also took her to his attorney for further advice, *after* she had separated from her husband (the plaintiff herein) and filed suit for divorce.

The case of *Fronk v. Fronk*, 159 Mo. A. 543, is also interesting. In this case the court held that

"to make the parents of plaintiff's husband liable it is not enough, as in the case of a stranger, to show interference by them, as malice on their part will not be inferred; but it must be shown that their conduct was not such as should be characterized as a natural result of parental solicitude but amounted to a clear case of want of reasonable justification."

And quoting from 30 Corpus Juris, page 1130 (with annotated cases thereunder):

223

"And such immunity does not depend upon a request for advice from the child nor upon the soundness of the parent's judgment as to the necessities of the case."

By analogy, "a parent may lawfully receive and harbor his married child who comes to him to avoid ill treatment and marital difficulties, or in the case of a daughter, even assist her to leave her husband's home." 30 C. J., page 1131, Section 998 and cases therein cited.

And in an action for alienation of affections, the plaintiff has the burden of proving *all the essential elements* of his cause of action and in actions against parents of the alienated spouse the burden of proof is heavier than in some other civil actions. See 30 C. J., page 1135, Section 1004.

Another matter involved in the instant case arises out of a conflict of laws.

In cases of torts, such as this action, the place of the wrong committed is in the state where the event necessary to make an actor liable for an alleged tort takes place. And the question whether or not an act gives rise to civil liability for tort depends upon the law of the place where committed. And in order that such liability may be enforced in another forum, the act which is the foundation of the action must be actionable by the place where committed. *Alexander v. Penn Co.*, 48 Ohio St., 623; *Davis v. New York etc. Rd.*, 143 Mass. 301. See generally Torts, 38 Cyc., 545.

And there is no conflict in the decided cases on the point that so far as the right of action is concerned, it must stand, if at all, on the statute or law of the state where the alleged injury occurred, and not of the state where the redress is sought. And since the acts complained of were committed by the defendant while he was in the state of New York, the

law of that forum will prevail. And since by legislative enactment the state of New York has barred such a cause of action,
the same limitation will apply in Ohio, and other states.

We now consider the third matter by way of defense in
the within cause.

It will be recalled on September 14, 1937, the parties hereto
executed and delivered to each other mutual releases. By the
terms thereof, the plaintiff released and discharged the defendant from any and all liability of every nature which he had
against the defendant from the commencement of time to
date of signing said agreement.

It is contended by plaintiff that it was the intention of the
parties to settle the then pending law suit, which had nothing to do with the present case. That may or may not be the
case. But the fact remains that the present *right* of action
accrued, if at all, to the plaintiff *before* said date. The fact
that no mention was made of it at the time is immaterial.
Where persons have voluntarily settled their differences by
an accord and satisfaction, the courts will not reopen the controversy without a sufficient showing to invalidate the accord,
such for instance as fraud, mistake or duress.

And none of these elements have been shown.

Furthermore, in order that such accord and satisfaction as
was entered into between the parties herein does not express
the full intent of the parties, as is claimed by the plaintiff, then
he, the plaintiff, must first file his action, which may have
been done by way of reply to defendant's answer, seeking
reformation or rescission of same.

Furthermore, where an accord and satisfaction is fully executed, there can be no rescission without restoring or offering
to restore what has been accepted in satisfaction. *Van de*

Velden v. *Chicago* etc. *Rd.*, 61 Fed. 54; *Gould* v. *Cayuga County Natl. Bank*, 86 N. Y. 75.

By reason of all of which the motion for a new trial herein filed is hereby overruled.

This decision supposedly came before one of the Judges of the Municipal Court of Cleveland. However, inquiry developed that there was *no such case on the docket*; that the trial judge had faked the parties to the action, which was *totally imaginary*; and that even the names of the parties, number and date, were figments of the Court's mind. Had not an alert newspaper reporter unearthed this phony opinion in time, it would have remained in the permanent records of published *Ohio Opinions*. The whole story was a complete fabrication. Such a judicial fairy tale has not been matched anywhere.

On June 10, 1754, the testimony of a ghost was admitted in evidence by the Edinburgh High Court of Justiciary. The famous legal historian, William Roughead, reports the incident in his *Twelve Scott Trials*. It came about in this way. One Sergeant Davies was murdered near Aberdeen in 1749. Nine months later, witness Alex McPherson talked with Davies' ghost and learned the name of the murderer. At the trial, what the ghost told McPherson was actually admitted in evidence. This is thought to be the only case in legal history where such testimony was allowed.[5]

THE BARBER AND HIS TOOLS

In *Terry v. McDaniel*, 103 Tenn. 415, the Supreme Court of Tennessee, speaking through Judge Wilkes, had the following to say about some articles belonging to a barber:

"This is an action of replevin. It originally involved a barber's chair, a looking-glass and a map of the world. After the battle of Manila and the close of the Spanish-American war the map of the world was released, presumably because it had become incorrect, obsolete, and valueless. The contest over the chair and the looking-glass, like the war in the Philippines, still continued, however, . . . The plaintiff says that he is a barber by occupation, and that he allows his customers to sit in the chair and look into this glass while he proceeds to make gentlemen of them, and these, with his razor, are tools of his trade or occupation and are exempt to him as a mechanic. . . . It is argued that no one is a mechanic except a person who works on wood or metal, but it is replied that the barber works upon the head and upon the cheek, so that, while there is a distinction between the two, it seems to be a distinction without any material difference. Attention is called to the fact also that frequently the impression made on the customer's face is similar to that made by a carpenter with his saw. This appears, however, to be owing more to the razor than to the chair or the mirror, but (for prudential reasons, no doubt), the constable did not seize the razor. . . . We think also, that, at his request, he must be classed as a mechanic and laborer, as well as orator and news-agent, and is therefore within the spirit of the law, and is entitled to the exemption."

A GOLFING JUDGE

Another decision, rendered in 1937 by Judge Perry T. Allen, of the Springfield (Missouri) Court of Appeals, contained the following discourse on golf:[6]

"Golf is an ancient game, known as the royal and ancient game of the Scottish Kings. It was first played in continental Europe in the early part of the Seventeenth Century, and about the middle of the Seventeenth Century was introduced into Scotland and found favor in the reign of James the Fourth. The game was played with a ball made of feathers and covered with leather, and played with rough, crude clubs, but presumably with the same feeling of frustration that accompanies its play in modern times. It is a game of precision, fraught with uncertainties, and yet, despite its uncertainties, the canny Scotch have indulged in it for centuries and introduced it to the unenlightened races. . . . Golf is a game of exact precision, requiring perfect coordination of mind and body. The slightest deviation of the club head from a perfect position, during the stroke or swing, will cause the

228

golf ball to do many peculiar things. It is apt to slice, it is apt to pull or hook, or travel straight at an angle, with neither hook nor slice. It does not require an intimate knowledge of the principles of geometry to know that a slight deviation of the club head may send the ball from the tee at an unusual angle. No player has ever achieved such perfection in the game that he does not occasionally hook or slice a ball. With ordinary players, as the evidence shows in this case, this frequently takes place. To hold that a golf player was negligent merely because the ball did not travel in a straight line, as intended by him, would be imposing upon him a greater duty of care than the Creator endowed him with faculties to carry out."

A BEGGAR AND HIS LEGS

In November, 1932, a beggar by the name of Josef Ballo sued for personal injuries in the District Court of Debreczin, Hungary. The evidence showed that he had lost one leg in an earlier accident, and the court refused to award damages for the lost of the other leg (which he lost recently in a railroad accident) because the judge believed that the accident placed Mr. Ballo in a better position for begging.[7]

A CORPORATION'S ALIENATION OF AFFECTIONS

In December, 1933, John L. Walsh, a Brooklyn Judge, ruled that a corporation could be sued for alienation of affections. One Louis Gold had sued Pocket Brassiere Co., Inc., et al, for two hundred thousand dollars, claiming that the officers of the defendant company had connived with one another and lured Mrs. Gold back to her old job, thereby ruining the plaintiff's life. A favorable decision was entered for the plaintiff, the corporation being held liable for alienation of affections.

PARROTS AND CONTRACT BRIDGE

One of the oddest decisions rendered by a New Jersey Court is found in *K. G. O. Construction Company v. King,* 171 Atl. 164. It was decided February 24, 1934, and reads:

"This is an action by the plaintiff (landlord) against the defendant (tenant) for nonpayment of rent alleged to be due it for an apartment rented to the defendant by the plaintiff under a lease. The defendant claims he owes nothing because he was forced to vacate his apartment before the lease expired on account of the screechiness and the annoying loquacity of a parrot owned and kept by another tenant adjoining his apartment which disturbed the peace and quiet of his home life. It is further contended by the defendant that a clause in the lease executed between the parties hereto forbidding the habitat of domesticated animals in the apartment house in question was for the benefit of the tenant, and that it became and was the duty of the landlord to cause the

230

said tenant to vacate or to forfeit said tenant's lease or to compel him to get rid of or in some way suppress the cause of the annoyance to the quiet enjoyment of the defendant's home.

"The court finds as follows: 'At first blush' as the Poet Pope might say, this is a case that could be appropriately designated in the language of our immortal Shakespeare 'Much ado about nothing,' but the earnestness of counsel and the parrot's continual interference with the processes of thought on the part of some or most of defendant's guests while playing at the delightful pastime contract bridge, plus the fact that the constant screechiness of the parrot might entail a loss of money to either party, have constrained the court to give it an unusual amount of attention.

"The court took great pains to delve into the legal tomes of this state for the purpose of discovering the exact legal or judicial status of a parrot. It failed to find any judicial so-called 'cause' of the trouble in the case. And in order to prevent some other judge from growing pale while ransacking our court decisions from its very beginning to the present time, this court does now hereby solemnly declare that a parrot is a domesticated animal.

"The court doth further find that the parrot in question was very screechy, querulous, and extremely loquacious, though not given (*mirabile dictu!*) to indulging in profane or indecent language. . . . The parrot, in this regard, had been well trained. Its foster parents had given much time, effort, and thought to its proper bringing up. In their zeal-ousness to make the parrot the talkative member of the family, they had forgotten in their education of him to teach him some of the nicer requisites of our present day social customs.

"In this day and age it is not good manners for a bystander or onlooker to interrupt or interfere in a card game, particu-

231

larly so if it is contract bridge. And to speak much above a whisper is not to be tolerated from anyone, much less an animal who has had heretofore no judicial or legal status.

"The court finds that the parrot was ill-mannered in disrupting the train of thought of the card players, and that when the parrot attempted continuously to speak above the voices of the players themselves, he brought himself within the realm of judicial censure.

"The court cannot refrain from judicially reprimanding the foster parents of the parrot for neglecting to teach the parrot when and when not to speak, or when and when not to inject his inharmonious, raucous and monosyllabic words upon the unlistening ears of pensive and serious-minded card players. *This penchant to break up card games on the part of this particular parrot or on the part of social parrots in general is judicially frowned upon.* The court finds the conduct of the parrot and its foster parents in this case was grossly indiscreet and eminently anti-social.

"The court regrets very much that these facts, important as they may seem to be, are not sufficient in law to render a verdict for the defendant but finds itself constrained by the laws of this state to find for the plaintiff on the ground that the landlord is not responsible for the acts of a third party tenant.

"The court further finds that the clause in the lease forbidding the habitat of domesticated animals in the apartment house by any tenant under pain of forfeiture of the lease was put in the lease by the landlord, and was for his own particular benefit and certainly not for the benefit of the defendant (tenant) in this suit, nor for the other tenants who might have occupied the apartment house in question at the time complained of.

"The court finds, therefore, that there is due the plaintiff,

K. G. O. Construction Company from the defendant George
W. King, Jr., the sum of $130.00 and costs."

In *Frank Epple* v. *The State*, 112 Tex. Crim. 612, 18 S.W.
(2) 625, the accused had been tried for transporting intoxicat-
ing liquor. Eight pints of corn liquor were found inside the
upholstery of his car. It was contended that some stranger

had suddenly left the whisky in the defendant's car. In adopt-
ing the opinion of the Commission of Appeals, the Texas
Court of Criminal Appeals said, on page 614:

"The appellant's theory seems to have been that this
stranger had in some way found a mysteriously hidden re-
ceptacle in the upholstering of his car and played him the
mean trick of filling it with whisky. Like a cuckoo bird, this
unfeathered follower of Bacchus surreptitiously slipped a
whole settin' of eggs into appellant's nest, after which he
was apparently swallowed up by space, leaving his trouble-
some brood to be hatched by another. We believe in Santa
Claus all right, but we confess the increasingly frequent appearance of this same stranger in Dido and Aeneas. This

233

ubiquitous disciple of John Barleycorn seems to have a peculiar habit of hovering around places just prior to their raid and search by officers, and then as mysteriously evaporating as the mists of an April morning. Unlike the roaring lion seeking whom he may devour, this omnipresent individual moves with the silent tread of a fairy and the swiftness of the lightning stroke, and over practically the entire state there have come complaints of his victims."

NOT GUILTY BUT ESCAPED

In 1877, the Supreme Court of Kansas rendered an opinion which stands unique in the list of reported cases. The decision itself will cause no particular stir, but the poetical report found in the Kansas records is most peculiar. The case involved the question whether one (accused of a crime of which one is later acquitted) violated a penal statute by escaping prison while waiting trial. To use the words of the Court: [8]

"The defendant claims that as he was acquitted on the charge of burglary, therefore that he did not commit the offense of escaping from said jail 'before conviction' upon said charge of burglary. We think otherwise. His offense, of escaping from said jail, comes as we think, within the letter and spirit of the statutes prohibiting escapes. He escaped from imprisonment for an alleged burglary, and had never been convicted of such burglary. His offense therefore comes within the exact letter of the statute, and of that section of the statute under which he was prosecuted. He escaped 'before conviction.' His offense also comes within the spirit of the statute."

From page 266 of Vol. 19 of the Kansas State Reports:

The State v. Lewis.

* REPORTER'S NOTE.—The peculiar features of the foregoing case of *The State v. Lewis*, seem to justify the inserting here of the "poetical report" thereof written by EUGENE F. WARE, Esq., attorney-at-law, of Fort Scott, and which he published in the "Fort Scott Daily Monitor," of 10th March 1878. Mr. Ware's "report" is as follows:

IN THE SUPREME COURT, STATE OF KANSAS.

GEORGE LEWIS, Appellant, ads. THE STATE OF KANSAS, Appellee.

[Appeal from Atchison county.]

SYLLABUS:

Law—Paw; Guilt—Wilt. When upon thy frame the law— places its majestic paw—though in innocence, or guilt—thou art then required to wilt.

Statement of Case, by Reporter:

This defendant, while at large,
Was arrested on a charge
Of burglarious intent,
And direct to jail he went.
But he somehow felt misused,
And through prison walls he oozed,
And in some unheard-of shape
He effected his escape.

Mark you, now: Again the law
On defendant placed its paw,
Like a hand of iron mail,
And resocked him into jail—
Which said jail, while so corraled,
He by sockage-tenure held.

235

Then the court met, and they tried
Lewis up and down each side,
On the good old-fashioned plan;
But the jury cleared the man.

Now, *you* think that this strange case
Ends at just about this place.
Nay, *not so.* Again the law
On defendant placed its paw—
This time takes him round the cape
For effecting an escape;
He, unable to give bail,
Goes reluctantly to jail.

Lewis, tried for this last act,
Makes a special plea of fact:
"Wrongly did they me arrest,
"As my trial did attest,
"And while rightfully at large,
"Taken on a wrongful charge.
"I took back from them what they
"From me wrongly took away."

When this special plea was heard,
Thereupon The State demurred.

The defendant then was pained
   When the court was heard to say
   In a cold impassive way—
"The demurrer is sustained."

Back to jail did Lewis go,
But as liberty was dear,
He appeals, and now is here
To reverse the judge below.

The opinion will contain
All the statements that remain.

Argument, and Brief of Appellant:
As a matter, sir, of fact,
Who was injured by our act,
Any property, or man?—
Point it out, sir, if you can.

Can you seize us when at large
On a baseless, trumped-up charge;
And if we escape, then say
It is *crime* to get away—
When we rightfully regained
What was wrongfully obtained?

Please-the-court-sir, what is crime?
What is right, and what is wrong?
Is our freedom but a song—
Or the subject of a rhyme?

Argument, and Brief of Attorney for The State:
When THE STATE, that is to say,
We take liberty away—
When the padlock and the hasp
Leaves one helpless in our grasp,
It's unlawful then that he
Even *dreams* of liberty—
Wicked dreams that may in time
Grow and ripen into *crime*—
Crime of dark and damning shape;
Then, if he perchance escape,
Evermore remorse will roll
O'er his shattered, sin-sick soul.

237

Please-the-court-sir, how can we
Manage people who get free?

Reply of Appellant:
Please-the-court-sir, if it's *sin*,
Where does *turpitude* begin?

Opinion of the Court. PER CURIAM:
We—don't—make—law. We are bound
To interpret it as found.

The defendant broke away;
When arrested, he should stay.

This appeal can't be maintained,
For the record does not show
Error in the court below,
And we nothing can infer.
Let the judgment be sustained—
All the justices concur.

[*Note by the Reporter.*]
Of the sheriff—rise and sing,
"Glory to our earthly king!"
[*E. F. W.*

SOURCES

Chapter 13

1. Jones on Evidence (3rd Ed.), p. 70; 1 Chitty, Pleading (6th Ed.), p. 258.

2. *State v. William Linkhaw,* 69 N. C. 214.

3. *U. S. v. 350 Cartons of Canned Sardines,* No. 7595, District Court of Western Pennsylvania.

4. *Wm. N. Selig* v. *George Fabyan*, reported in file B-19054 (April 21, 1916), in the office of the Clerk of the Circuit Court, Cook County, Illinois.

5. Twelve Scott Trials, by William Roughead, p. 85.

6. *Page* v. *Unterreiner*, 106 S. W. (2) 528 at 533.

7. Docket of the District Court of Debreczin, Hungary (November, 1932).

8. *The State of Kansas* v. *George Lewis*, 19 Kansas Report 260.

CHAPTER 14

LEGAL GEMS

"Old Father Antic—the Law."
—William Shakespeare

THE CODE OF HAMMURABI

IN THE Louvre Museum in Paris stands an eight-foot column of marble. For thousands of years it stood on the outside wall of Babylonia warning all who entered the temple gate that they were "presumed to know the law."

Chiseled on this pedestal were some three hundred fields of law, enforced by Hammurabi, a famous Mesopotamian king, who reigned twenty-three hundred years before Christ. Some of the law provisions found on this rare piece constitute present-day law. According to Dean John Wigmore, it represents the earliest national code ever found in the world.[1]

Unearthed in 1902 by a French archeological commission working near Susa, Persia, the stone was removed to France where it may now be seen on exhibition. It is known as the Code of Hammurabi and is considered the greatest treasure of Babylonian law.

241

THE CASE OF THE CAT'S LEGS

A British court sitting in India rendered the most amusing opinion ever given on proximate cause. In 1880 a cat was bought by four men, each of whom agreed to own a separate leg of the cat. Soon after, the cat hurt one of its legs and the owner of that limb bound it up with a rag soaked in oil which subsequently caught fire. The cat rushed in among some cotton bales jointly owned by the four men and set them on fire. The three owners of the unhurt legs sued the other for the value of the goods consumed. The owner of the injured leg denied liability and counterclaimed. The Court said:

"The cat could not use the injured leg; it held it up and ran with the three others. These three carried the fire to the cotton and alone are culpable. The owners must therefore compensate the defendant for his loss."[2]

THE DOGHOUSE CLUB

An up-to-date legal gem is the charter which was granted May 18, 1937, to the Doghouse Club, Inc. of Cleveland. It is on file in the office of the Secretary of State in Columbus, Ohio. The Articles of Incorporation of the club, which is described as "a social, charitable and fraternal organization," list its purpose as being "to establish and maintain clubrooms to shelter married men when domestic and civil fury makes it necessary for them to seek refuge away from home."[3]

STRINGS TIED TO JUDGMENTS

Strings were actually tied to judgments in the fifteenth century by the Indians who inhabited what is now Peru. History

tells us that before the Incas were exterminated by the Spaniards they had developed many arts. Although they possessed no system of writing, they did keep records of their legal disputes by knotted strings. All evidence of this unique method of recordation was done away with, however, when Pizarro and his Spanish followers conquered Peru.[4]

SPAIN'S LONGEST LAWSUIT

In Spain a lawsuit involving fees for drafting a poll-tax register lasted 728 years. This is supposed to be the longest lawsuit not only in the history of Spain but in the entire world. It dates back to 1167. The parties that started suit claimed compensation for compiling a poll-tax register at one of the villages of the Republic of Andorra. Upon the death of the original parties, their next of kin kept the suit alive.

Final disposition of the case was made by the Barcelona Court of Appeal in 1895, which found in favor of the parties who brought the action.[5]

LAWYERS' NAMES

Some of the best legal "queeriosities" are found in the names of law firms. In 1880, *Ketchum and Cheatham* was a well-known New York firm. In order to avoid undesirable publicity, the name was changed to *I. Ketchum and U. Cheatham.* Their first names really were "Israel" and "Uriah."[6]

Abel Crook was a prominent Manhattan lawyer.

A group of lawyers who recently practiced in Akron were named *Dilly, Daly, Doolittle and Stahl.*

Other firm names adding to the gaiety of the legal profession are *Argue & Phibbs* of Ireland, *Wind & Wind* of Chicago, and *Stahl, Stahl, & Stahl,* a practicing firm of reputable lawyers in Port Clinton, Ohio.

THE HIGHEST MONEY JUDGMENT

The highest money judgment ever awarded was entered on March 6, 1922, in the Superior Court of Santa Clara, California. It was for an amount in excess of three hundred trillion dollars. The exact figure is shown in the illustration.[7]

This unprecedented award came about in this way. George Jones had bought a considerable quantity of feed for his live-stock from Henry B. Stuart of San Jose, California, so on January 18, 1897, Jones signed a one-hundred-dollar note payable to Stuart and gave it to him as security for the feed bill. The note bore ten per cent interest per month, compounded monthly. Years went by, and nothing was paid on

245

the note. At last Stuart felt he had waited long enough, so he ordered his lawyer to reduce the note to judgment. Outside accountants were hired to compute the amount of the judgment. A hearing was had before Judge J. R. Welch of Santa Clara who entered the stupendous judgment. On May 2, 1922, execution was returned and filed, the record showing a credit of only $19.69 having been paid by Jones on the judgment. Since that time, it has been reported that the defendant has gone through bankruptcy. No wonder!

A PIG POEM

A firm of attorneys in Williamsburg, Kentucky, filed an amusing answer in McCreary Circuit Court some years ago. It seems that one Andrew J. Hamlin owned a hog which was run over and killed by a train belonging to the Cincinnati, New Orleans & Texas Railway Company. Suit was filed for damages against the company which, through its firm of Tye, Siler, Gillis & Siler, answered as follows: [8]

> Poor Andy had a hungry hog,
>   And feed was high, you know;
> So anywhere it pleased to jog
>   He let it freely go.
>
> It strayed upon the railroad track
>   Just as a train came by;
> It heard the bell and roar and clack,
>   But never cocked an eye.
>
> Before the greatest human skill
>   Could stop the speeding train,

With one last thought of seas of swill,
Poor pig was cut in twain.

This foolish shote was just a runt
While eating Andy's feed,
But since it gave its final grunt
Behold! it's pedigreed.

COURT HUMOR

Even laymen will concede that once in a while courts manage to display a sense of humor, by getting off such remarks as the following:

"But Women will talk, for God has made them so."
Richardson v. Roberts, 23 Ga. 215 at 221.

"For a man to swear while trying to button his shirt collar is not to be regarded as a sympton of softening of the brain."
Keithley v. Keithley, 85 Mo. 217, at page 224.

In *DeVide* v. *DeVide*, 186 N. Y. App. Div. 814 (1919), it was held at pages 817 and 818 that one isolated instance of a husband's throwing a pair of shoes at his wife does not justify the granting of a decree of separation—*particularly if he missed.*

One of the most cynical thrusts was what the famous English Judge, Lord Holt, once said:

"Now, there is no manner of difference between a college and a hospital, except only in degree; a hospital is for those that are poor, and mean, and low, and sickly; a college is for another sort of indigent person; but it hath another intent, to study in, and breed up persons in the world, that have not

247

otherwise to live, but still it is as much within the reason of hospitals."

Philips v. *Bury*, 2(eng.) Term Reports (1788) 346 at p. 353.

JUDGES ON DELICATE SUBJECTS

Quite infrequently judges write decisions on imaginative and delicate subjects. A few choice bits have been discovered.

In *Rutherford* v. *Hobbs*, 63 Ga. 243, Judge Bleckley said at page 245:

"John Doe is a mere figment of the law's imagination, with no more existence as a real suitor than Mercury has as a real God. Only during high poetic transport does the law regard him as a true objective personality. Though born of the muse, he is dry and commonplace enough to be engaged in the extensive real estate business which he pretends to carry on, but in very truth, he is a phantom—a legal will o' the wisp, an ingenious conceit of the law in its rapt poetic moods."

An Indiana judge announced Biblical history when he observed in a reported case that:

"Immediately after the fall of Adam, there seems to have sprung up in his mind an idea that there was such a thing as decency. . . . And it historically appears that . . . the first exercise of mechanical ingenuity was in the manufacture of fig leaf aprons by Adam and Eve, by which to conceal one from the gaze of the other."

Ardery v. *State*, 56 Ind. 328 at 329.

Judge Logan E. Bleckley of the Supreme Court of Georgia discreetly said in the case of *Neal* v. *State*, 64 Ga. 272 at pages 274 and 275:

248

"And what can be more fit than for the court to send out a juror, attended by a bailiff, when he is under a stress of nature which civilized man regards as a summons to retire? A comparison of the various possible methods of meeting and dealing with such an emergency had better be left to silent meditation than discussed here with needless realism. It is enough if those who may become interested in the subject will form a mental picture of the situation, and contemplate it for themselves."

WORDS IN LITIGATION

It may be hard to believe, but each of the following words has been the center of litigation at one time or another:[9]

a	for	the	after	that
an	from	till	also	then
about	in	to	as	unless
at	like	under	but	when
before	near	until	either	where
below	of	unto	if	wherefore
besides	off	up	nor	whether
beyond	on	with	or	while
by	over	within	so	whilst

COMIC-STRIP CHARACTERS

Various comic-strip characters have had their day in court. "Buster Brown,"[10] however, was the first to be drawn into litigation. Next came Fred Opper's creations, "Alphonse and Gaston."[11] Then followed "Mutt and Jeff,"[12] "Barney Google," and "Spark Plug,"[13] and recently "Betty Boop-a-Doop."[14]

In the case of *Richardson v. Coca Cola Bottling Company*, in the Superior Court of Baltimore City, Judge O'Dunne said on May 20, 1938:

"It is claimed that the doctrine of '*res ipsa loquitur*' applies to the facts of this case. There is no such *doctrine*. It is a pious symbol, long used by priests of the law to exorcise spirits. It is some of that ancient and sacred legal nomenclature which means nothing more than a statement that the obvious is self-evident. If the thing itself speaks, let it talk English! If a barrel of flour rolls out of a second story warehouse window and falls on the head of a passerby it is not the self-rising quality of the flour that made it jump out of the window and crown the forgotten man heedlessly passing below. The facts suggest that someone in the warehouse was negligent in leaving the door open, and the barrel on its side instead of on its head—therefore let him respond in damages for so doing, or prove he did not do so. Even where such so-called rule is applied, it is limited to instances where exclusive control is in the defendant. . . ."

In the 17th chapter of a book by Stuart Chase on *The Tyranny of Words*, he discusses legal words that might well be eliminated from the law. I nominate "*res ipsa loquitur*" for execution by the firing squad, and ask that it be shot at sunset without the formality of further trial.

EPIGRAMMATIC JUDGES

Oftentimes, judges let fall remarks which are good epigrams.

"Common sense is always good law, but law is not always common sense."

                Medlin v. *Balch* (Tenn.) 52 S.W. 140 (1899).

"When a man becomes a lawyer, he does not have to lose his wits."   *Harland* v. *Territory*, 13 Pac. 453.

"The fact that a lawyer advises foolish conduct does not relieve it of its foolishness."

                Hanscom v. *Marston*, 82 Me. 288 @ 298.

"Counsel's misapprehension of the law, *however natural*, is not ground for setting aside the conviction."

                People v. *Voelker*, 221 N. Y. Sup. 760 @ 767.

"An attorney has no right to be a clam and shut himself up in the seclusion of his own self-conceived knowledge of the law. He must keep pace so far as reasonable diligence and a fair amount of common sense will enable him to do so with the literature of his profession and what the courts have decided."   *Hill* v. *Mynatt*, (Tenn.) 59 S.W. 163 @ 167.

Judges, on the other hand, do not want to be divorced from the profession entirely, as illustrated by what one Court recently said:

"While there has been feeble suggestion that a judge is no longer a lawyer, it is not denied that one elevated to the bench is no longer an *attorney at law*."

                Soda v. *Marriott*, 130 Cal. App. 589.

One of the choicest bits of wisdom appears to have been entered by an English judge who said:

"No attorney is bound to know all the law. God forbid

that it should be imagined that an attorney, or a counsel or even a judge, is bound to know all the law."

Montrion v. Jefferies, 2 C. P. p. 116.

A WITTY OPINION

A truly witty opinion was rendered by the late Judge Oliver H. Bloodworth in *City of Atlanta* v. *Sciple*, 19 Ga. App. 694. He said:

"In passing it might not be out of place to remark that, should tax returns of many of our 'good men and true' be conclusive as to the value of their property, numbers of fortunes in the state would shrink and shrivel even as a ripe plucked fig when exposed to a summer sun."

ALL THE LAW AND THE GOSPELS

In discussing the authorities submitted by counsel in the case of *Stephens & Co.* v. *Alberts*, 256 Pac. 15, the Colorado Supreme Court said:

"So far as we have been able to determine, the diligence of counsel has spread before us all the 'Law and the Gospels' touching the question at issue. Four chapters of the Bible, department bulletin No. 1151 of the United States Department of Agriculture, Belden on Fur Farming for Profit, Harding on Fox Raising, Darwin's Origin of Species, Shakespeare's Henry IV, St. John Lucas, Suetonius, Aesop's Fables, the Tale of the Spartan Youth, the Harvard Law Review, the Albany Law Journal, the Central Law Journal, the London Law Times, the Criminal Law Magazine, and certain anonymous writers, not to mention numerous statutes and court decisions, adorn and illuminate their briefs."

TRADEMARKS

A certain trademark was denied registration. The Chicago lawyer representing the applicant submitted this brief:

"Ivory is a good trademark for soap not made of ivory. Gold Dust washing powder is not made of gold. Old Crow whiskey is not distilled from crows. There is no bull in Bull Durham. Royal Baking Powder is not used exclusively by royalty, nor is Cream Baking Powder made of cream. Pearline contains no pearls, and White Rock is water. There is no cream in cream of tartar, in cold cream or in chocolate creams, no milk in milk of magnesia, in milkweed or in cocoanut. These are all as remote from the cow as the cowslip. There is no grape in the grapefruit or bread in the breadfruit. A pineapple is neither pine nor apple; and an alligator pear is neither pear nor an alligator; and a sugar plum is not a plum. Applebutter is not butter. All the butter is taken out of buttermilk, and there is none in butternuts, or in buttercups, and the flies in the dairy are not butterflies."

SUPREME COURT GEMS

The Supreme Court of Maryland said in *Barnes* v. *State*, 41 Atlantic 781, 783, that a court does not judicially know what "monkey business" is.

In *Tolin* v. *Terrell*, 117 S.W. 290, the Supreme Court of Kentucky held that one is contributorily negligent in going behind a mule without first speaking to the animal.

The case of *Reniger* v. *Fogossa*, reported in I Plowden, p. 13, which was decided in the fourth year of the reign of King Edward VI before the Justice of the Exchequer, Earl of Wilt, Sir John Baker and the Justices of England, announced:

"that a statute, which punished a prisoner as a felon who broke prison, did not extend to a prisoner who broke out when the prison was on fire, 'for he is not to be hanged because he would not stay to be burned.' "

The United States Supreme Court has referred to this many times.

LINCOLN ON TOO MUCH TALK

The comment made by President Lincoln concerning misconduct of counsel should not be omitted from a survey of legal gems. Lincoln had served only a few years at the Illinois Bar when he found himself pitted against a lawyer who was quite garrulous. When it came time for argument, opposing counsel shook, waved his arms and persisted in going far outside of the record. Lincoln's reply began:

"My friend who has just spoken to you would be all right if it were not for one thing, and I don't know that you ought to blame him for that, for he can't help it. What I refer to is his reckless statements without any ground for truth. You have seen instances of this in his speech to you. Now the reason of this lies in the constitution of his mind. The moment he begins to talk, all his mental operations cease, and he is not responsible. He is in fact much like a little steamboat that I saw on the Sangamon River, when I was engaged in boating there. This little steamer had a five-foot boiler and a seven-foot whistle, and every time it whistled the engine stopped."

THE AMIABLE JUDGE SUTHERLAND

An amusing order was written by Judge Josiah Sutherland of the New York Supreme Court. It ran as follows: [15]

"After hearing of counsel, no one appearing in opposition thereto,

IT IS ORDERED that the following officers of the Supreme Court appear with the said Josiah Sutherland, Justice of the Supreme Court, at one o'clock on the afternoon of this day, at Delmonico's restaurant and partake of a champagne lunch at his expense; and the said officers of said Supreme Court as aforesaid are hereby notified that if they or any of them fail to obey the order they will be adjudged guilty of contempt of Court and punished to the utmost extent of the law."

WINDOW BLINDS

A window blind is considered to be real estate, if hung. This is one of the present-day legal gems. Leading authorities on the law of property do not hesitate to advance the proposition that window blinds are not personal property, but real estate, when hung up in a building.[16]

In 1924, the late Charles Merrill Hough, a well-known Federal district judge sitting in New York, wrote some comments *Concerning Lawyers*. Speaking of lawyers' tricks and technical devices as divulged when they talk shop, he said:

"This inexhaustible fund of tales of shrewdness (to use the most reputable name) marks the average practicing lawyer as one who learned young and never forgets to be clever and quick, and not too scrupulous for his client. He is rarely original, is usually content to show that the same thing has been done before . . . and before he passes middle age is positively resentful of novelty either in thought or action. There are some practicing lawyers, possibly a hundred in the whole United States, who are not parasites. . . . They (the others) have no independent existence; they think, move and have their beings as substitutes for their clients. Most lawyers are timid to the last degree in doing anything that may appear unpopular. . . . The general body of lawyers are perfectly worthless even in choosing judges. . . . Whenever a friendly cutie looks for evidence of literature, culture or broad learning of any kind among actively practicing lawyers, who must dominate the profession because they live by it and with it, he finds not near enough to leaven a lump of any size, much less a body of a hundred thousand men. . . . 'The attorney mind' . . . is roused to shrewdest activity only by being employed to do somebody else's business. It is never auto-dynamic; it seems as static as a copper wire until the current of a retainer flows through—then it is active enough, and even dangerous, for many of the most skillful lawyers seem unaware of the effect of their vigor as is a current-carrying wire."

In conclusion:

"If it were possible to practice law without being enslaved by clients and acquiring the attorney mind, which is essentially a slavish mind, practice would be perfect, but, as that cannot be, my conclusion is that any lawyer may enjoy independence in thought and social action, if he will refrain from client serving; but few of them can, and still fewer try; so that most of the tribe are, long have been, and probably will remain, a clever, agreeable, servient class, not over-scrupulous about winning cases, quite pleasantly careless about their own affairs, jacks of many trades and usually masters of none —not even their own. A curious compound which I cannot approve nor urge upon others; yet for myself, I have enjoyed it all."[17]

Obviously Judge Hough's comments apply to only a very few of the many lawyers practicing in the United States.

TWELVE MEN GOOD AND TRUE

One of the greatest legal gems, although it is not a part of the law itself, is an old English song entitled *Twelve Men Good and True*. It describes most juries of the past centuries.

> The rusty key has whined in the lock,
>   The rickety door is fast.
> They are shut inside with their irksome job
>   Left to themselves at last.
> A dozen chairs and a rough deal board,
>   And a curtain rung askew—
> And here they'll hide till they can decide—
>   The twelve men good and true.

257

A prisoned bee in the hot sunlight
    Jumps on an upper pane,
His low monotonous mumble set
    To a garrulous, grim refrain,
"Guilty or not? Guilty or not?"
    The heavy hours lurch by.
They nick the table with idle knives
    And shift their quids and sigh.

Up in the dusty jury room
    The frantic bee falls dumb.
A yawning watcher seals its doom
    With a flick of a calloused thumb.
"Guilty or not? Guilty or not?"
    They fidget with their trust
A free man soon, or in a moon,
    A dangling sack of dust?

Eleven in line—one hanging back
    An old saw in his head,
"Let Us make man, Let Us make man,"
    Something the Lord God said.
Scrape of a chair, thump of a boot
    He feels for his hat with a frown.
"Have it your way—I've said my say.
    "Look ye, the sun is down."

Eons gone, with His own strong hands,
    And in His own strange plan
Back in the red, dim dawn of Time,
    Brooding, He made him, man.
In His own splendid image wrought;
    Then when the frame was whole,
Breathed in his nostrils the Breath of Life,
    And lo! a living soul!

The rusty key has groaned in the lock,
A scuffling tread's on the stair.
The wise judge offers his hooded ear.
His words drop slow and spare.
"Hanged by the neck until dead" spake he,
"Make way and let them through
"They're tired now and they want their tea,
The twelve men good and true."[18]

SOURCES

Chapter 14

1. Panorama of World's Legal Systems, by John Wigmore, Vol. I, p. 87.

2. Leading in Law and Curious in Court, by Benjamin F. Burnham, p. 755.

3. Office of the Secretary of State, Columbus, Ohio.

4. Panorama of the World's Legal Systems, by John Wigmore, Vol. III, p. 1125.

5. Records of Barcelona Court of Appeal (1895).

6. Salad for the Solitary and the Social, by Frederick Saunders, p. 437.

7. Henry B. Stuart v. George Jones, No. 27,579, Santa Clara Superior Court.

8. Hamlin v. Cincinnati, New Orleans & Texas Railway Company, McCreary Circuit Court, Kentucky.

9. English in the Law Courts, by M. M. Bryant.

10. Empire City Amusement Co. v. Wilton (1903), 134 Fed. 132.

11. N. Y. Herald v. Star Company (1906), 146 Fed. 204, aff'd 1023.

12. N. Y. Herald v. Ottawa Citizen, 41 Canada S. C. R. 229.

13. Hill v. Whalen (1914), 220 Fed. (D. C.) 359.

14. Star Company v. Wheeler Syndicate (1916), N. Y. Law Journal (August).

15. Celebrated Trials, by Henry L. Clinton, p. 344.

16. The American Law of Real Property, by C. G. Tiedeman (4th Ed.), p. 12.

17. The William Feather Magazine, October, 1939.

18. 15 Ohio Law Reporter 81.

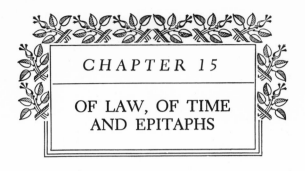

CHAPTER 15

OF LAW, OF TIME AND EPITAPHS

"A 'shyster' is the other fellow's lawyer."
—Walter Winchell

THE HONEST SOLICITOR

IN LONDON, on a tablet in the north aisle of the Church of St. Dunstan, lies a curious epitaph. It reads:[1]

"Hobson Judkins, Esquire, late of Clifford's Inn, the Honest Solicitor who departed this life, June 30, 1812. This tablet was erected by his clients as a token of gratitude and respect for his honest, faithful and friendly conduct to them throughout life. Go, reader, and imitate Hobson Judkins."

A LOVER OF PEACE

Richmond Church contains a monument, with a whimsical epitaph, to the memory of Robert Lawes, Esq., who, though a barrister, "was so great a lover of peace, that when a contention arose between Life and Death, he immediately yielded up the ghosts to end the dispute."[2] Apparently this peaceful soul chose the wrong profession.

261

Here lies an honest lawyer and that is
Strange

A JADED JOKE

In 1929, attorney George W. Biddle of the Mansfield,
Ohio Bar, contributed to the *Ohio Law Reporter* the following poem entitled "A Lawyer AND an Honest Man":

The story's been told to make folks laugh
Of a lawyer dead whose epitaph
Was so composed that the wording ran:
"Here lies a Lawyer, an Honest Man."
An Irishman said as he drew near:
"Sure it must be two are buried here."

The story tho good the first time told,
With much re-telling grew trite and old;
Yet seldom failed some mirth to provoke—
This jaded and time-worn lawyer joke.

A lawyer who with a lunch club dined
Heard it so often he lost his mind;
From hearing it told as speakers do—
The wormy old chestnut just like new.

Non compos mentis but having pride
He covertly plotted homicide—
He'd slay the next teller of that yarn
And bury the corpse behind the barn!

He whetted his ax and oiled his gun,
Ate raw meat daily just for the fun;

Went to luncheons as customary
And sought the man he'd kill and bury.

In advance an epitaph he wrote,—
You re-hash orators please take note.
All budding humorists be forwarned
By these lines which that man's slab adorned:

Here lies the body of one who died—
By now he's toasted, roasted or fried;
He lent his voice to idle rumor
Which proved he owned no sense of humor.

A lawyer who held his honor dear
Felled him and planted his body here;
The mortal who thus put on the ban
Was a lawyer and an honest man.[4]

A BAD BEGINNING

There is a story in Washburn's *Judicial History* that the first lawyer who came from England to practice in Boston was sent back because he was caught tampering with a jury.[5]

CLIENT V. LAWYER

Eccentric epitaphs concerning law have not been confined to lawyers; clients have left some amusing ones. One reads:

When we've nothing to dread from the Law's sternest frown
We all laugh at the barrister's wigs, bags and gowns;
But as soon as we want them to sue or defend,
Then their laughter begins, and our mirth's at an end.

A friend of the legal profession once observed that:

All Lawyers Go to Heaven
   Regardless of Their Worth—
For the Very Simple Reason
   That They Catch Their Hell on Earth.

A contemporary answered:

The man that wrote that poem may have known a thing
   or two
But if lawyers go to Heaven they are mighty, mighty few.
There never was a class of men in valley, dale or dell,
More qualified to scrap it out among themselves in Hell.

Laymen sometimes forget that most lawyers remain friendly with one another despite the most bitter court fights. The famous poet, Saxe, sagely observed:

Two lawyers, when a knotty case was o'er,
Shook hands, and were as friendly as before.
"Zounds," said the client, "I would fain know how
You can be friends, who were such foes just now?"
"Thou fool," said one, "we lawyers, though so keen,
Like shears, ne'er cut ourselves, but what's between."

The feelings of many laymen are perhaps best expressed by the poem which was published in the *Albany Journal* years ago. It was called "The Client's Plea" and ran this way:

Who taught me first to litigate,
My neighbor and my brother hate,
And my own rights to overrate?
   MY LAWYER.

Who cleaned my bank account all out,
And brought my solvency in doubt,
Then turned me to the right-about?
MY LAWYER.

In turn, the answer on behalf of the lawyers left nothing to the imagination.

Who lied to me about his case
And said we'd have an easy race,
And did it all with solemn face?
MY CLIENT.

Who took my services for naught,
And did not pay me when he ought,
And boasted what a trick he'd wrought?
MY CLIENT.

So there are two sides to this eternal dispute which wages so furiously between clients and lawyers—sometimes seriously, but most times jokingly, thank fortune!

"Law, lawyers and judges have their faults," said the Hon. John C. Knox at the Sixty-First Annual Meeting of the New York Bar Association,

"but, let our critics, if they will—search the ends of the earth for a land where right and justice prevail to a greater extent than here—in America, where we with all our frailties give sponsorship to the rule of just law and decent living."

REMBRANDT

It has been reported that the great artist Rembrandt was discharged from bankruptcy two hundred and sixty-one years after he had died.[6] Hence nobody should become disheartened at the thought of dying insolvent; some heir will undoubtedly have the records expunged so as to erase the blot on the escutcheon and thus save the family name.

NEVER TOO OLD TO BE PUNISHED

Donald McDonald, of Boston, Massachusetts, was convicted of being a common drunkard when he was 103 years old. In September, 1825, the *Boston Courier* carried the story concerning this real Scotch verdict. McDonald, a resident of Boston, was brought before the local magistrate, charged with intoxication. After giving the case due deliberation, the Court convicted the accused of the charge and in the entry declared him to be a "common drunkard," having been such for one hundred and three years.

In the illustration following, the one epitaph beginning, "Here lies justice," appeared on the headstone of a magistrate who had formerly been a barber.[7]

266

CONCLUSION

"The task is ended, and aside we fling
The musty books tied up with legal string;
And so good night, since we our say have said,
Shut up the volume and proceed to bed;
And dream, dear reader, of a future, when
A lawyer may shake hands with you again." [8]

SOURCES

Chapter 15

1. Tablet in Church of St. Dunstan, Fleet St., London, England.

2. Law and Lawyers, Curious Facts and Characteristic Sketches, by David L. Purves, p. 83.

3. Oddities of the Law, by F. F. Heard, p. 121.

4. 30 Ohio Law Reporter 597.

5. Bouvier's Law Dictionary, Vol. 1 (1879 Ed.), p. 97.

6. 29 Illinois Law Review, p. 990.

7. Law and Lawyers, by Irving Browne, p. 297.

8. Legal Facetiae, by Willock.

INDEX

Above Ground, 133
All the Law and the Gospels, 252
All Trains Stopped Permanently, 184
Amiable Judge Sutherland, The, 254
Ancient Wills, 123
Animal Beneficiaries, 138
Animal Defender, 205
Another Long One, 209
Arizona Arrest, An, 96
Author Forced To Eat His Own Words, An, 91

Bacon's Punishment, Roger, 86
Bad Beginning, A, 263
Ballad on Wills, 154
Barber and His Tools, The, 227
Bear Jury? A, 37
Becket, Thomas A, 45
Beggar and His Legs, A, 229
Beggar Monrousseau, 15
Bentham's Will, Jeremy, 128
Bequeathed Dinner, A, 134
Bidwell Gang in London, The, 59
Bigamist's Punishment, A, 76
Blackstone, William, 206
Blue Law and a Monkey, A, 40
Book Burning, 85
Boorn Brothers Case, The, 20
Bull of Adrian, The, 188
Bull Murderer, A, 37

Captain Kidd's Execution, 54
Cardinal Wolsey's Punishment, 90

Case of the Cat's Legs, The, 242
Change in Pi, A, 183
Christmas Prohibited, 187
Christmas Prohibited in Massachusetts, 187
Clause for Lawyers, A, 153
Client v. Lawyer, 263
Cloth Check, A, 106
Code of Hammurabi, The, 241
Cold-Water Trial, The, 175
Christopher Columbus' Trial, 58
Comic-Strip Characters, 249
Compurgation, 171
"Concerning Lawyers," 255
Conclusion, 267
Congressional Record Honors a Georgian, The, 192
Consider Your Verdict, 71
Consistency—Hobgoblin of Judges, 78
Convicted of Self-Murder, 18
Convictions of Cows, 37
Corporation's Alienation of Affections, A, 230
Courageous Judge, A, 211
Court Filibuster, A, 203
Court Humor, 247
Crime To Kill Fairies, 186
Criminal Roosters—1938, 39
Crude Wit, 69
Cynical Provisions, 135
Cruikshank's Bank Note, 108

Damages for Barking Dogs, 219
Deeded to God, 97
Deeded to Jehovah God, 99
Defiant Will, A, 146

Demosthenes, 199
Disputed Identity, 50
Disraeli, 208
Dissent, 131
Distribution of Lawyers, 190
Disturbing Singer, A, 214
Dixon's Irony, Chief Justice, 196
Doghouse Club, The, 242
Drake's Brass Plate, Sir Francis, 102
Dred Scott Decision, The, 55
Drink the Sea, 131
Drumheads, 151
Dutch Nation Indicted, The, 58

Eccentricity v. Insanity, 127
Eels' Rights, 30
Egotism, 200
Egyptian Mummy Case, The, 49
Epigrammatic Judges, 250
Estate Willed to Lord Jesus, 122
Expensive Bonfire, An, 108
Excommunication of Doves, 30

Family Revenge, 162
Feminine Embellishments Forbidden,
    188
Field, Stephen John, 201
Floral Rentals, 130
Food in English, 195
Food Restrictions, 188
Forfeit of "Mister," 86
Free Bite, A, 166

Galileo's Perjury, 60
German Petty Offenders, 85
Golfing Judge, A, 228
Grasshoppers and a Dead Lawyer, 32
Guarded Beard, A, 148
Guillotiner Guillotined, The, 87

Haymarket Square Case, The, 61
Head Baskets, 84
Head Plowing, 77
High Cost of Law, The, 71
Highest Money Judgment, The, 245
Highwayman Judge, 207

Honest Solicitor, The, 261
Hoss Sense, 67

Idol Heir, An, 152
Imaginary Law Suit, 221
Intentionally, 133

Jaded Joke, A, 262
Joan of Arc as Lawyer, 60
Job's Will, 124
Judges' Gems, 218
Judges on Delicate Subjects, 248
Judges Penalized, 185
Judgments from His Bed, 204
Juries Then and Now, 165

Kansas Automobile Statute, 183
Knife Trials, 171

Land Limitations, 184
Law-Phobia, 210
Lawyers Can Cry, 217
Lawyers' Fees, 210
Lawyers' Names, 244
Leap Year Enforced, 187
Leeches Brought to Justice, 30
Libelous Will, A, 139
Light Forever Burning, A, 132
Lincoln's Defense of Innocent "Mur-
    derers," 22
Lincoln on Too Much Talk, 254
Longest Civil Case, The, 62
Longest Question, The, 209
Lover of Peace, A, 261

Massachusetts Blue Laws, 189
Massachusetts Punishments, 90
Metal Bridle, The, 83
Method for Civil Cases, A, 169
Methuselah of the Law, 214
Milk Drinking, 86

270

"Neck Verse," The, 160
Never Too Old To Be Punished, 266
Noah's Ark Exploration Association, The, 114
No Complaint Without a Witness, 163
No English Authorities, 194
No Funeral Bell, 133
No Funeral Expense, 146
No Manual Labor, 185
No Witnesses, 162
No Women Smokers in New York, 191
Not a Farthing If They Married, 135
Not Guilty But Escaped, 234

Oaths, 170
Original Pole-Sitters, 79

Parrots and Contract Bridge, 230
Patient v. Doctor, 58
Penalized for Extravagant Apparel, 81
Penn's Punishment, William, 87
Penalties of Jurors, 80
Penalty of Silence, 77
Penalty Without Crime, 76
Persistence, 206
Petticoat Will, 140
Philpotts Changes His Name, Mr., 114
Phonograph-Record Evidence, 153
Pigs on Trial, 34
Pig Poem, A, 246
Pledges of John Hedges, The, 137
Plowshare Punishment, 82
Poetic Brief, A, 106
Poetic Will, 134
Pope Formosus, 44
Preserved Organs, 151
Preserved Skulls, 150
Pressing for an Answer, 88
Price of a Wife in Virginia, The, 189
Prohibition of Beards, 186
Property Traced to Adam and Eve, 110
Prosecuted Horses, 38
Punishment of the Chinese Idols, 82
Punishment of Huguenots, 85
Punishment of Marble Statues, 82
Punishment That Made a Lawyer, The, 89

Rats!, 210
Rats Up for Burglary, 35
Razor-Back on a Railroad Track, A, 117
Reasonable Doubt, The, 72
Recent Animal Convictions, 40
Rembrandt, 266
Required Drunkenness, 185
Retroactive Marriage License, A, 113
Revenge in a Will, 122
Rifle Sentenced, A, 88
Roman Views on Wills, 124
Rooster Sorcerer, The, 32
Rope Justice, 53
Roquefort Cheese Requirements, 186
Roulette Winnings, 50

Sacrilegious Donkey, A, 38
Sadism?, 92
Saint Ives, 200
Sanctuaries for Criminals, 158
Self-Defense, 68
Seven-Year Trial, A, 60
Shakespeare Not the Author, 220
Shakespeare's Will, 132
Shortest Charges, The, 70
Smallest Check, 196
Smallest Real Estate Transaction in History, The, 118
Smoker's Will, A, 147
Socrates v. Athens, 61
Spain's Longest Lawsuit, 243
Steel Check, 104
Strange's Epitaph, Sir John, 262
Streets Blocked by Churches, 187
Strings Tied to Judgments, 243
Supreme Court Gems, 253
Suspense, 137

Testimony of a Ghost, 227
Texas Court Believes in Santa Claus, 233
Thirty Sous to Cats, 139
Thou Shalt Not Bear False Witness, 81
Threatened Greek Legislators, 80
Tichborne Imposters, The, 51
To a Clean-Shaven Son, 136

Trademarks, 253
Transfer of Property, 164
Traveling on the Sabbath, 84
Trespassers "Persecuted," 93
Trial by Bier, 168
Trial by Combat, 176
Trial by Hot Water, 173
Trial of the Ants, The, 29
Trial of the Mosquitoes, The, 29
Trial of the Weevils, The, 28
Trials of Caterpillars, Locusts, Flies and
    Crickets, 29
Twelve Men Good and True, 257
Twenty Thousand Death Sentences,
    207
Two-Volume Complaint, A, 106

Unconscious Lawlessness, 194
United States Legal Measure, 189
United States v. 350 Cartons of Canned
    Sardines, 216

Voltaire's Punishment, 87

Walker's Trousers, Mary, 191
When Is a Lawyer a Fish? 194
White Linen Clothes, 129
Whole Town a Judge, The, 163
Will in Shorthand, A, 153
Willed to the Dead, 136
Williston Fish Will, The, 144
Wills of Famous People, 126
Wills on Eccentric Materials, 141
Window Blinds, 255
Wittiest Judge, The, 66
Witty Opinion, A, 252
Woman-Hater's Will, A, 149
Wooden Check, A, 105
Words in Litigation, 249
Women Who Quarrel, 78
Work or Die, 79
World's Largest Political Meeting, The,
    208
World's Longest Deed, The, 109
World's Longest Lease, The, 104

Yorick's Skull, 150